WALKING THE WORLD'S
NATURAL WONDERS

WALKING THE WORLD'S
NATURAL WONDERS

First published in 2008 by
New Holland Publishers (UK) Ltd
London • Cape Town • Sydney • Auckland

www.newhollandpublishers.com

Garfield House
86–88 Edgware Road
London
W2 2EA

80 McKenzie Street
Cape Town 8001
South Africa

Unit 1, 66 Gibbes Street
Chatswood, NSW 2067
Australia

218 Lake Road
Northcote
Auckland
New Zealand

10 9 8 7 6 5 4 3 2 1

ISBN 978 184537 762 5

Editorial Direction: Rosemary Wilkinson
Commissioning Editor: Ross Hilton
Designer: Isobel Gillan
Cartography: Stephen Dew
Production: Marion Storz

Reproduction by Pica Digital Pte Ltd, Singapore
Printed and bound by Tien Wah Press Pte Ltd, Singapore

The authors and publishers have made every effort to ensure that all
information contained in this book was correct at the time of press. They
accept no responsibility for any loss, injury or inconvenience sustained by
any person using this book or the advice given within it.

The sketch maps in this book are intended to illustrate the journeys
described in the text. They should not be used as a substitute for accurate
cartography in the field.

Front cover Sossusvlei Dunes, Swakopmund, Namibia
Page 1 Eucalyptus forests, Blue Mountains, New South Wales, Australia
Pages 2–3 Dawn from Gilman's Point, Kilimanjaro, Tanzania
Pages 4–5 Rhino Peak, Drakensberg Mountains, South Africa

CONTENTS

FOREWORD by Benedict Allen

PREVIOUS PAGE *Desert south of Jebel Khasch, Wadi Rum Protected Area, Jordan*

Some years ago, whilst walking in the Rift Valley of Kenya, I came across a young Maasai herder. 'We can walk together,' he said, simply. Leaving his thorn-bush corral, his beloved cattle and their clouds of flies, he led me towards what looked like a very promising escarpment. 'No doubt there's a spectacular view from up there,' I thought. 'He wants to show it me.' Together we scrambled up out of the dusty plain, and the scene which now revealed itself was indeed impressive. Below us lay an ancient red earth rug scattered with gazelle and zebra; acacias were quietly grazed by giraffe and, in the far distance, a lone elephant was nudging a tree to shake off fruit. But we didn't stop for long. The boy was intent on going further – and we were still walking many hours later.

There was, I began to understand, no destination. The Maasai herdsman was walking purely for the sake of it – as I had been, earlier that morning. We shared the same motivation, it seemed: that primeval pleasure to be had from simply putting one foot in front of the other so as to feel the world unfold around you. Yes, there would be the splendid views, those unexpected vistas which reward the uphill slog. But there'd also be the chance encounter – the startled mongoose, the unexpected creek and its water-dancing insects - we'd be embraced by huge, cloud-laden skies, taste the sweet tang of herbs on the breeze. Such are the plethora of surprising, enlivening moments which, on any such walk, combine together in some ancient chemistry to heal the soul.

This book could not be more timely. Never has our planet seemed more precious; never has there been a greater urgency for us to savour it. And what better way to understand our place in the higher scheme of things than to leave behind our isolating homes and cars, and take a walk. How I envy the author Jon Sparks the sights, smells and sounds that must have come his way whilst compiling this volume. Some of these lands I know well – reading the following pages I've found myself again transported to the high steppe of Mongolia, the skylarks burbling in the blue skies. And I found myself again in Namibia, plodding with my camels through mountainous dune seas with the southerly wind on our backs, while in the

8

△ Pausing to consult the map. Benedict Allen in the Skeleton Coast, Namibia

desert sands below our feet were scattered the ostrich shell necklaces of Bushmen, the bones of miners lured to their death by the promise of diamonds. I recalled too hiking alone up onto the plateau of Roraima, where, in the mist, I laid a trail of thread through the labyrinth of contorted black rocks to ensure I'd find my way back down again.

The reader of this book should not need a thread to guide him safely home – he has these pages as a trusty guide. But the great thing is that, even without setting foot anywhere, you can flick through these pages and find yourself on a journey of the imagination, striding through the exquisite wilderness, enriched and humbled by the thought of the innumerable natural wonders still to be encountered out there.

INTRODUCTION

"I see Earth! It is so beautiful!"

YURI GAGARIN

△ *Salto Ángel (Angel Falls), Venezuela*

The first glimpses of the Earth from space changed things forever. Perhaps it was the end, or the beginning of the end, of the era of exploration for humanity as a whole. But for each individual, the world is still waiting to be explored, and maybe it is more important than ever that we do so.

The view from space is awesome, but ultimately detached. To understand what it means we need to explore the Earth at ground level, and there is no better way to do so than on foot. Walking is the most natural, the most primeval way of getting about. Walking pace allows the world to unfold and reveal itself. Walking allows all the senses to engage. Walking takes us into a landscape, while other modes of transport detach us from it. The philosopher Nietzsche said, 'only those thoughts that come by walking have any value.'

On every continent, in every age, in vastly different ways, people have expressed their wonder at the great spectacles of nature. The great volcanoes of New Zealand's Central Plateau were held so sacred by the local Maori that passers-by had to shield their eyes. And on Australia's Larapinta Trail, especially with a good guide, you can get a shadowy inkling of the profound relationship between the Aboriginal people and the land.

Natural marvels inspire myths and stories everywhere. The medieval hero Roland is said to have hewn a cleft through the mountains with his sword Durandal: this startling gash in a Pyrenean ridge is still called *la Breche de Roland*. And legends continue to grow: Conan Doyle's 'Lost World' was inspired by Roraima in Venezuela.

Wonder does not just reside in the great show-pieces. There is also something to marvel at in the curve of a sand-dune, the miniature world of a rock-pool, or a splash of green moss in the black volcanic deserts of Iceland. A journey on foot is about much more than arrival at a single destination.

If great natural wonders excite and inspire us with awe, they should also strengthen our resolve to treat with respect not only the great sites but also the natural world as a whole. The overarching principle is to leave minimal trace of your presence. In this, too, walking is unbeatable, only equalled by a few other means of transport, like canoeing and cross-country skiing.

While walking itself has minimal impact, getting to the starting points of the walks is a different story. It's no longer possible to ignore the fact that visiting these places involves a lot of travel, which typically means flying. How do you balance the environmental negatives of long-haul flight with the economic benefits that responsible tourism can bring, or the possibility – for example – that national park fees paid by trekkers help to sustain environments that might otherwise fall prey to deforestation?

It's a complicated equation. Perhaps, rather than focusing solely on the 'carbon footprint' of a single journey, what matters is our overall impact throughout our lives. If close encounters with the world's natural wonders provoke a greater sense of the world's beauty, fragility and interconnectedness, there is much to gain.

For every place included in this book, there are legions more that equally inspire wonder; the marvellous South Island of New Zealand, the hauntingly beautiful islands of the Hebrides, the crystalline distances of the South American Altiplano. Still, every walk in this book embodies something special. In all their diversity, they have one thing in common, reminding us that the world is dynamic and ever-changing. Nature is a work in progress.

Nowhere is this clearer than in active volcanic regions, from Hawaii to Iceland and New Zealand, where 'as old as the hills' becomes nonsense: the hills may be younger than you are. Other walks take us back through the dizzying spans of geologic time. England's Jurassic Coast, Newfoundland's Gros Morne National Park, and the Burgess Shales of British

▽ *Path in Vallee de Pouey Aspe, Pyrenees, France*

Columbia all bear prime significance for human understanding of the way the Earth was made, and continues to evolve.

The Burgess Shales yield fossils from the first great blossoming of life on Earth. Today's living world – complex, often fragile and sometimes endangered – is the overriding theme of many of the walks. It might be the abundance of Brazil's Atlantic rainforest that inspires awe, or the ability of life to thrive in apparently hostile environments, whether close to the Arctic Circle in Finland or in the dunes of the Namib Desert.

If some walks reveal the volcanic and tectonic processes that build up the Earth's crust, others are dominated by the evidence of erosion, from great river canyons like the Verdon or the Grand Canyon to the grinding glaciers of the Himalaya, Alps and Andes. The stark valleys and ridges carved by vanished glaciers are the headline story in areas like Newfoundland and Norway.

If the areas visited are diverse, the walks themselves vary widely in their level of challenge. However, all should be within the grasp of any reasonably fit person who prepares sensibly. There's no need to carry huge loads, or to scale sheer precipices.

Some areas are covered by day-walks, but most of the walks in this book last from three to ten days. All the European walks are possible without camping, thanks to an abundance of snug mountain and wilderness refuges, supplemented by village inns. Of course, camping is an attractive alternative, allowing a deeper relationship with the environment, though in some protected areas it may be banned or restricted.

Outside Europe, camping is the norm for most trips. However, every walk in this book is covered by companies which provide fully supported trekking (we mention, in passing, a few that aren't). This normally means that walkers only need carry a light day-sack, while everything else is transported by porters or pack-animals or – occasionally and regrettably – by motor vehicle.

The levels of challenge still vary widely; the specific chapters give greater detail, but each individual must interpret this in light of their own experience. A particular challenge, and potential risk, is posed by altitude. Several of the walks spend time above 4,000 m (13,125 ft), with the highest point being the summit of Kilimanjaro at nearly 6,000 m (20,000 ft), where the air pressure is only half its sea level value. While a good level of basic fitness certainly helps, there is no substitute for acclimatization, allowing the body to adapt gradually to altitude.

In general the walks do not pose great technical difficulties; there is no need for rock- or ice-climbing skills. However, several do venture into exposed situations where a good head for heights is required. Rough edges and unpredictability are intrinsic to the natural world. It demands respect, and rewards it magnificently.

▷ *Trekkers in Ormiston Gorge, Larapinta Trail, Northern Territory, Australia.*

EUROPE

"To be surprised, to wonder, is to begin to understand."

JOSE ORTEGA Y GASSET

△ *La Rondiella, Picos de Europa, Spain*

Europe is an idea, rather than a physical fact: geographically it is contiguous with Asia. But somehow its significance outweighs all that. Europe has an unrivalled capacity to surprise. It may be the smallest continent (unless you count Australia) and the most densely populated, but it has an extraordinary diversity of environments and habitats. From its most southerly point at Tarifa in Spain, to Nordkapp in Norway, continental Europe stretches over more than 35 degrees of latitude. There are active volcanoes, major glaciers and ice-caps, neck-stretching precipices and plains that reach further than the eye can see. Europe has most of the deepest (known) caves in the world and one country alone, Norway, has three of the world's ten highest waterfalls.

Europe's diversity is extended even further by stretching a point to include some significant islands. Iceland is culturally European, but geologically it is something else, the place where the mid-Atlantic Ridge breaks the ocean surface. Further away still are the Canary Islands; geographically they belong to Africa, but politically they are part of Spain.

Europe's diversity, combined with its relative compactness, means that widely differing environments are often spanned by modest journeys. These can mostly be made without flying, allowing the traveller to stay connected with the changing landscape. This is perfectly exemplified in Britain, where a day's journey spans almost the entire geological history of the earth. The science of geology has deep roots here, and the Jurassic Coast is arguably the single most influential geological location on the planet.

Europe is also the most walker-friendly continent, both because of its terrain and because walking, for necessity and for pleasure, is deeply embedded into European culture. It's where walking for recreation really began, and across most of Europe there is a well-developed infrastructure of walkers' buses, waymarked paths and welcoming refuges. This is at its very best in the Alpine states, and in Scandinavia.

Scandinavia also sets the gold standard for freedom to roam. The traditional 'Every Man's Right' allows free passage on foot almost everywhere, and even the right to camp on most land. Similarly enlightened legislation has recently been implemented in Scotland too (England and Wales lag some way behind). Elsewhere in Europe these rights may be more circumscribed but there are many rights of way and *de facto* freedom to roam often prevails, especially above the tree line.

Europe's geography, and much of its history, pivot around the Alps, shared by half a dozen nations. The Walkers' Haute Route is a fine introduction to the range, starting in the shadow of their highest peak and ending in sight of their most iconic, the Matterhorn. At the far end of the Alpine chain, the Dolomites are one of the most uncompromisingly spiky ranges on Earth.

The Pyrenees are a walker's range *par excellence*, where few peaks or passes require crampons or a pre-dawn start. Further west, Spain's Picos de Europa are a compact block of mountains, cramming a lot of verticality into a small area.

Western Europe's largest country, France, uniquely claims a share of both Alps and Pyrenees, and also has many dramatic landscapes all its own, nowhere more so than where the herb-scented hills of Provence are cleft by the Verdon Gorge.

Europe may be the most crowded continent, but it has its quiet places. Bulgaria's Rodopi Mountains are a shining example, with a relatively undeveloped character and an abundance of wildlife. For true wilderness, however, look to the far north. Finland is the most hospitable place on earth to venture beyond the polar circles. In summer there is round-the-clock daylight, in winter the magical experience of the Northern Lights.

Last but not least, Norway's fjords are one of the most exciting landscapes on Earth, but by their very (precipitous) nature don't always lend themselves to walking. But in the Jotunheim range good trails thread through wild rugged terrain dotted with hospitable refuges.

Of all the continents, Europe most seems designed for walking. Here, again and again, is magnificence without masochism.

▽ *Walker below the Breche de Roland, in the Pyrenees*

ICELAND
The Laugavegur Trail

JON SPARKS

△ *Geothermal springs*

Iceland is geology in action. Here the Mid-Atlantic Ridge, one of the most dynamic zones of the earth's crust, rears above the ocean surface like a breaching whale. Active volcanoes and hot springs abound and the country draws all its power and heating from geothermal sources. But it is also a northern land, dangling like a pendant from the Arctic Circle, and glaciers cover more than ten percent of the land area. The tag 'Land of Ice and Fire' may be a cliche but it is undeniably accurate.

The land is young and often bare; the scarcely-weathered rocks flaunt raw primary hues of red, yellow and black. Blue pools, white ice, and scattered, startling patches of green moss or huddled clumps of trees add to the kaleidoscopic palette of colours. It's impossible to take it all in on a short visit, but one of Iceland's most popular treks, the Laugavegur Trail, makes a fair attempt.

The trek starts at Landmannalaugar; there are natural hot pools, but ask before bathing as there have been reports of infection. The way winds through a gorge then climbs to the hot springs of Storihver, set among multicoloured lava flows. The trail continues across expanses of black, glassy obsidian to the Hrafntinnusker Hut. The hut draws hot water from a nearby steam vent which emits a constant jet-engine roar.

It's quite feasible to push on from here and combine the first two days into one, but it seems better to allow more time to absorb the extraordinary landscape. From Hrafntinnusker you can also take a side trip to an ice-cave melted out of a glacier by more steam vents.

Beyond Hrafntinnusker the views begin to open up to the south, towards the great ice-caps of Myrdalsjokull and Eyjafjallajokull. The trail passes countless hot springs, steam vents and pools of boiling mud. Patches of moss are almost shocking in their lurid green. Finally you descend to Alfavatn (Swan Lake) and the second hut.

From Alfavatn the route passes the volcanic cone of Storasula, daubed green with sheets of moss, and forges across the dark desolation of Maelifellssandur with its braided streams, of which several must be forded, towards the abandoned pasture-lands of Emstrur.

PREVIOUS PAGE
Landmannalaugar, Iceland

After a night at Emstrur the trail follows deep painted canyons and there are some exposed paths perched above wild glacial rivers. Hand-lines are usually in place on the steep, loose, slopes approaching the bridge over the grey, roaring Sydri-Emstruá. There's one final river to wade before Þórsmörk; knee-deep, fast and stunningly cold, it's best crossed in a group.

Þórsmörk means 'Thor's forest' and it's a very special place for Icelanders; a verdant, sheltered oasis in a land where there are more hot springs than trees. Birch trees shiver in the breeze and flowers sprinkle the level meadows.

▽ *Myrdalsjokull Glacier, Iceland*

▷ *The 60m (200 ft)*
Skógafoss waterfall

facts and figures

DESCRIPTION: 4 days' walking across rugged mountain terrain, surrounded by glaciers and volcanic activity

LOCATION: the southernmost region of Iceland

WHEN TO GO: mid-July to mid-September is best, but August can be very busy; pre-booking of huts is essential

START: Landmannalaugar, served by scheduled buses from Reykjavík

FINISH: Þórsmörk, bus service to Reykjavik. Extension to Skógar, also with bus service to Reykjavik

DURATION: 5 days (4 nights); optional extension adds 2 days

MAX ALTITUDE: 1,020 m (3,346 ft) at Fimmvörðuháls pass

ACCOMMODATION: simple, cosy mountain refuges

SPECIAL CONSIDERATIONS: huts have mattresses and stoves but walkers must carry sleeping bags and all food. Some organised treks will ferry baggage between huts. Be prepared for extremely changeable weather. Trekking poles are useful for stream crossings

PERMITS/RESTRICTIONS: camping permitted only near huts

GUIDEBOOK: *The Rough Guide to Iceland* by David Leffman, pb Rough Guides

After a final night in the Þórsmörk hut, there are several options for the last half-day. A short climb to the hill Valahnjukur gives a good view over the valley, while the Stakkholtsgja canyon hides a lovely waterfall. Even the ride back to Reykjavik is hardly tame, as the bus fords axle-deep through glacial rivers that you'd hesitate to tackle on foot.

As an extension to the trek, you can also cross the Fimmvörduhals to Skógar. This 23 km (14.3 mile) route can be done in one long day but is better spread over two. A sharp ridge leads up onto the stony table-land of Morinsheii. You can overnight at the Fimmvörduskáli hut, often reached by crossing an ice-bridge over a river, or continue straight on to the Fimmvörduháls pass. On the far side of the pass there's a snow-field; late in the season this can turn to bare ice seamed with small crevasses. Just beyond is the alternative overnight halt at the Baldvinsskali hut. From here you follow a dirt road for 5km then descend alongside the Skóga river, which spills over a succession of waterfalls. They're all dwarfed by the 60m (200 ft) Skógafoss just before the end. Skógar has an intriguing little folk museum with recreated turf houses, and a bus service to Reykjavik.

▽ *Rain shower on the Laugavegur trail near Emstrur Hut*

OULANKA NATIONAL PARK
Karhunkierros Trail

JON SPARKS

F inland stakes a fair claim to being the world's most northerly nation, with a quarter of its territory north of the Arctic Circle. Winters are long and dark, relieved by the unearthly brilliance of the Northern Lights, but summer days are endless. Finland's northern regions are thinly-populated yet well-serviced and accessible, and the Finns know more than most about making themselves comfortable whatever the conditions. In the vast northern spaces, wolves still prey on the reindeer herds.

▽ *Looking down from Kallioportti*

One of Finland's most popular hiking trails is the Karhunkierros, or Bear's Trail. This runs for most of its 80 km (50 miles) length through Oulanka National Park, which exemplifies the northern landscape of forest, crag and waterfall. Brown bears still forage in the deeper recesses. Summers explode into flower and autumn is rich with berries and fungi; thanks to 'Every Man's Right' (Finnish: *Jokamiehenoikeus*) these can be freely picked.

Karhunkierros can be walked in either direction, but is more commonly taken north to south. It divides naturally into three sections, with road access in between. Strong walkers could tackle each section in a day, but it's more usual to spread the trip over four or five days. Wilderness huts, shelters and camping places are spaced along the trail.

△ *Evening view from Ruka Fell*

The northern starting point is Hautajärvi, just a few kilometres south of the Arctic Circle. The opening stretches run through dry, open pine forest; in lusher patches the ground-cover flames red in autumn. In the Savinajoki gorge the trail passes the natural rock sculpture of Rupakivi, reminiscent of an Easter Island statue. About 15 km (9.3 miles) from Hautajärvi the Savinajoki meets the Oulanka river at the lake of Savilampi. The steep-walled Oulanka Canyon is just upstream. The Savilampi wilderness hut is a good place to spend the first night, lulled to sleep by the ceaseless river.

An hour downstream the river is re-crossed on a swaying suspension bridge overlooking the Taivalköngäs rapids; there's another wilderness hut nearby. It's another 8 km (5 miles) along the river to the Oulanka Visitor Centre, where there's a choice of campsites (with cabins). If the bustle's too much you can push on downriver about 6 km (3.7 miles) to the next wilderness cabin at Ansakämppä.

Climbing away from the visitor centre, there's a bird's eye view of the foaming Kiutaköngäs rapids. From here the trail follows cliff-tops. After Ansakämppä there's a great view of the Oulanka's tortuous windings before the trail climbs into the Kitkanniemi uplands, dotted with patterned swamps called *aapa* mires. There's a good lunch spot, or possible campsite, on the shores of the lake Kulmakkajärvi. Soon after this the trail drops to the Kitkajoki river, and threads a way upstream, first below the cliffs and then along their rim.

DESCRIPTION: 4–5 days' walking through wild forests and river gorges and over open fells

LOCATION: Oulanka National Park in the Kuusamo region of northern Finland

WHEN TO GO: approximately May – September, but some campsites etc. are only open June – August. Colourful and midge-free, September is the ideal time

START: Hautajärvi (bus service from Salla or Kuusamo)

FINISH: Ruka (same bus route)

DURATION: 4–5 days

MAX ALTITUDE: 491 m (1,611 ft)

ACCOMMODATION: wilderness huts. By doing the trail in three long days it is possible to use serviced campsites (with cabins) instead

SPECIAL CONSIDERATIONS: you need to carry a sleeping bag and food if using wilderness huts. These have fireplaces and wood, but a stove may still be useful. In summer take a good insect repellent

PERMITS/RESTRICTIONS: camping, fires, etc. only at approved locations

GUIDEBOOK: *Travellers' Finland* by Jon Sparks, pb Thomas Cook

Now there's a choice as the main Karhunkierros Trail meets its baby brother, Pieni Karhunkierros, which loops out from Juuma. The northern branch is shorter but involves a steep climb on wooden steps to the fine eyrie of Kallioportti. The southern arm is a little longer but takes in one of the finest sections of gorge on the whole trail. The waterfall of Jyrava is not high, but full of boiling malevolence. Above this is 1.5 km (almost a mile) of continuous rapids at Aallokkokoski, a favourite with rafting parties.

The two arms rejoin near the rapids of Myllykoski and then it's a couple of kilometres

out to civilization at Juuma, though you could skip this slight detour and press on; 7 km (4.4 miles) of fairly easy going through mire-dappled forest gains the next hut at Porontimajoki.

The trail now rises into bald, open fell country, warming up on the ridge of Kumpuvaara and then climbing onto the steep shoulder of Konttainen hill. There's one final climb onto the long ridge of Valtavaara, its highest point 491 m (1,611 ft) above sea level. After the days of forest and gorge the expansive views are intoxicating. Eastward, the forests roll off, almost uninterrupted, into Russia. Out to the west is a classic Finnish panorama, splashed with innumerable lakes (or not strictly innumerable: someone has counted, and there are officially 187,888 lakes in Finland).

The last descent may be tackled eagerly, or with reluctance; either way there's a sharp change of scene with the infrastructure of the ski facilities preceding Ruka itself. But there's beer, and pizza, and even, if you can handle it, a karaoke bar.

△ *Crossing the bridge at Niskakoski, near Juuma*

◁◁ *Jyrava waterfall*

JOTUNHEIMEN
Beneath the Hurrungane Giants

ANTHONY TOOLE

Carved by glaciers during the last Ice Age, Norway's longest and deepest fjord, Sognefjord, winds for 200 km (125 miles) from the coast. Its branching arms reach into Fjaerland, Naeroy and Aurland before it twists to an end through the gnarled fingers of Luster and Årdal. Its canyon continues for 40 km (25 miles), transformed into the country's deepest and most impressive valley system.

Utladalen has the Gothic symmetry of a cathedral. A full kilometre deep, its hanging valleys Stølsmaradalen, Midtmaradalen, Fleskedalen and Uradalen lead like transepts from the nave. Spires and flying buttresses rise to more than 2,000 m (6,565 ft) on both sides: Stølsnostind, Falketind and Uranostind to the east, and the Hurrungane peaks to the west, dominated by Store Skagastølstind, Norway's third highest peak.

From a bend in the Sognefjell road, just above Turtagrø, a good track leads gently along Helgedalen for 4 km (2.5 miles) and up to a pass and a signposted junction. Like most mountain tracks in Norway, this is marked, at intervals, with a large, red 'T' painted on a prominent rock. A much steeper track now zig-zags for 800 m (2,626 ft) to the 2,068 m (6,788 ft) summit of Fannaråken, on which stands the highest mountain hut in Norway.

The view from here extends across countless peaks to the north, then west to Lusterfjord and more distant mountains, capped by a shining Jostedalsbreen, Norway's largest ice sheet. To the south are the glaciers and jagged summits of the Hurrungane, the most Alpine of the peaks of Jotunheimen, where Norwegian mountaineering was born in the 1870s. From the eastern cliffs, the Fannaråken glacier runs down toward the head of Utladalen, from which the land rises again to central Jotunheimen, with Galdhøpiggen and its satellites marking the distant skyline.

The track from the hut follows the rim of the crags, then drops steeply to the Keisarpass. Before reaching the pass, a short detour to the 1,741 m (5,714 ft) summit of Keisaren gives a spectacular view of the east Hurrungane peaks, Gjertvasstind and Styggedalstind, and their glaciers, which crash over an icefall into Gjertvassdalen.

▽ *Fannaråken summit*

The lake below the pass, Gjertvatnet, is likely to be frozen, even in summer. From there, the track continues down Gjertvassdalen and into Utladalen. A wooden suspension bridge crosses the river, and a further 2 km (1.25 miles) of track picks its way southward through woodland, before opening out, quite suddenly, to reveal one of the finest and most beautifully situated huts in Jotunheimen, Skogadalsbøen.

A short distance east of the hut, a bridge over the river leads to a track that runs southward for 12 km (7.5 miles) along the high side of Utladalen, as far as Vetti, where it joins a road linking it to the eastern tip of Sognefjord. About 3 km (2 miles) from the hut,

OVERLEAF *The Hurrungane and Fannaråken from the notherly limit of Utladalen*

▽ *Gjertvasstind and Styggedalstind from Keisaren*

▷ *Skogadalsbøen*

this track is abandoned for a grassy 300 m (985 ft) ascent to Friken summit. At only 1,503 metres (4,933 ft), Friken is dwarfed by its neighbours, yet gives an unparalleled view across the profundity of Utladalen, which plunges for more than 1,000 m (3,282 ft), then rises with equal steepness, but to a greater height on the far side.

The walls and floor of Utladalen are covered by dense forest, in which bears were hunted until the early twentieth century. It was from a tiny refuge deep in this valley that British climber William Cecil Slingsby made a series of assaults on the Hurrungane peaks. Slingsby's ascent, in July 1876, of Store Skagastølstind is regarded as the birth date of mountaineering in Norway.

The track northwards from Skogadalsbøen re-crosses the suspension bridge, then continues into the upper, shallower reaches of Utladalen. After 7 km (4.4 miles), the track splits. The right fork is followed past a series of small mountain lakes to the watershed. To the south-west is a final view of the Hurrungane and Fannaråken. To the east lies the tongue of the Smørstabb glacier. A gentle descent for 2 km (1.25 miles) leads to Krossbu and the Sognefjell road.

▽ *Down Midtmaradalen to Utladalen and Stølsnostind*

DESCRIPTION: 4 days' walking on well-marked tracks in rugged mountain terrain, staying in mountain huts

LOCATION: the western end of Jotunheimen, Norway

WHEN TO GO: end of June to early September. Weather often very good, but be prepared for rain, and even the occasional snow shower

START: Turtagrø Hotel, Sognefjell road

FINISH: Krossbu Mountain Lodge, Sognefjell road

DURATION: 4 days, though Day 3 could be removed, or days added for further excursions from Skogadalsbøen

MAXIMUM ALTITUDE: 2,068 m (6,788 ft) on Fannaråken summit

ACCOMMODATION: 3 nights in fully-staffed huts – all meals provided

SPECIAL CONSIDERATIONS/EQUIPMENT NEEDED: snow patches will be encountered, though ice axes and crampons are usually unnecessary

PERMITS/RESTRICTIONS: membership of DNT (Norwegian Mountain Touring Association) recommended, though non-members may still use huts

GUIDEBOOK: *Walking in Norway* by Constance Roos, pb Cicerone Press

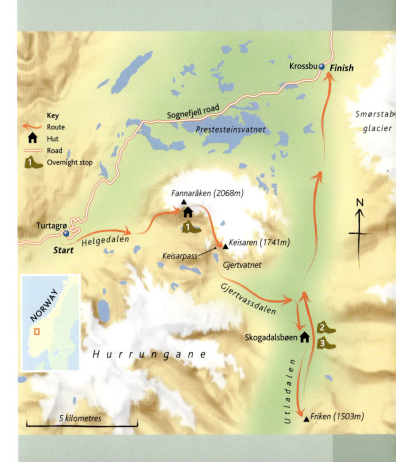

HAUTE PROVENCE
The Verdon Gorge

JON SPARKS

The Verdon Gorge is often dubbed the Grand Canyon of Europe and in French is officially called le Grand Canyon du Verdon. At around 20 km in length, it's not on the same scale as *the* Grand Canyon, but it's still impressive by any standards. The bed of the river lies around 600 m below the ridges, but what makes the Verdon stand out is its vertical and sometimes overhanging walls of grey limestone, up to 300 m high. These massive bastions of firm rock have made it one of the world's premier sites for rock-climbing, with over 1,500 recognized routes.

▽ *The Verdon River at Castellane*

Fortunately you don't have to be a rock gymnast to appreciate the Verdon, as there is a walkers' route, the Sentier Martel, which negotiates the most impressive section with the help of a few tunnels and ladders. This makes the Gorge the magnificent centrepiece of a walk across the rocky, herb-scented land of Provence; empty hills and lonely trails are often found on the other days, contrasting with the Gorge itself, with its inevitable honeypot buzz.

The opening day follows hill paths overlooking Lac de Castillon. In spring it's a floral delight, loud with bees, and you appreciate why this

△ *Griffon Vulture*

region is noted for its honey. The village of Castellane huddles under the abrupt outcrop of Notre Dame de Rocher, which commands great views over the rooftops and across the folded hills.

From Castellane follow the well-marked GR4 route (in its entirety this runs right across southern France) high above the deepening valley of the Verdon. For most of the way you're following a Roman road, passing several small villages which seem embedded in the rocky slopes, finally descending to Rougon. Just below the village is a not-to-be-missed viewpoint, aptly named Pointe Sublime, which has a dizzying prospect into the great gorge; either inspiring or intimidating as you contemplate the next day. The area around Rougon is also notable for the successful reintroduction of Griffon Vultures, which are regularly seen rising the thermals on their huge wings.

It's advisable to make a prompt start, as this is a long and quite strenuous day. Descending into the shadows of the gorge, you then follow the ingenious Sentier Martel, with its tunnels, ladders and bridges. Following the line of least resistance, the Sentier makes several significant climbs and descents within the gorge, so at times you're high above the green river but there are also places where you can swim in it. The tunnels were originally excavated for a hydro-electric scheme which was later abandoned. The first of these, the Tunnel du Baou, is the longest at over 600 m (1,970 ft). It's a relief to emerge

DESCRIPTION: 5 days' walking in the rocky hills of Provence, mostly easy but with a taxing and exciting day through the Verdon Gorge itself

LOCATION: the pre-Alps of Provence in south-eastern France

WHEN TO GO: ideally spring and autumn; possible in summer but very hot and busy

START: St. Andre Les Alpes, served by narrow-gauge train (Chemin de Fer de Provence) from Nice

FINISH: Riez; bus or taxi to Manosque where there is a railway station

DURATION: 5 days walking

MAX ALTITUDE: 1,380 m (4,528 ft)

ACCOMMODATION: village hotels and guest-houses

SPECIAL CONSIDERATIONS : take a torch for the tunnels of the Sentier Martel. The landscape is dry and the sun can be very hot: carry plenty of water

PERMITS/RESTRICTIONS: none

GUIDEBOOK: *Walking The French Gorges* by Alan Castle, pb Cicerone Press

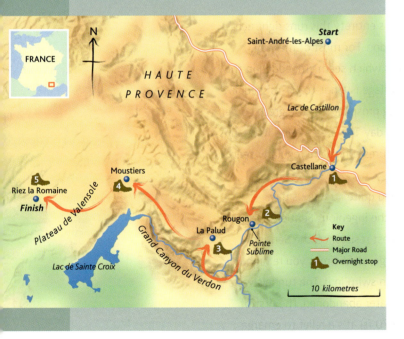

from the chilly darkness to the warmth of the day, and one of the most impressive sections of the gorge, where the walls of l'Escalès and l'Encastel confront each other.

As the day wears on the heat reflecting off the rock walls can be intense; sun-protection and a good intake of water (not from the river!) are needed. Good places to rest are the Baumes-Fères beach and the confluence of the Verdon and Artuby rivers at La Mescia. Here you can appreciate the turquoise hue of the water, which inspired the name of the river. The narrow passage of the Étroit des Cavaliers and then the graceful footbridge at l'Estellié signal the beginning of the end – apart, that is from the long switchback climb up to la Maline. From here it's still 8 km (5 miles) along the road to the overnight stop at La Palud and many weary walkers have opted to take a taxi.

After the confines of the gorge, the next day is refreshingly open, climbing through mixed forest to a high ridge at about 1,380 m (4,528 ft) and then descending through rocky, pine-scented forest to the little town of Moustiers, straddling a ravine and famous for its earthenware. The final day presents more contrasts, leaving the high hills for the softer landscape of the Plateau de Valensole, which is cultivated for lavender, grapes and apples. Patches of oak forest are exploited for the precious truffles. The final night is in the town of Riez la Romaine, mostly medieval but – as the name suggests – boasting a history reaching back to Roman times.

▷ *The Verdon Gorge is heavily forested*

THE PYRENEES
Gavarnie and Ordesa

JON SPARKS

If one natural wonder is ample justification for a good walk, how about three? Cirque de Gavarnie, Breche de Roland, Ordesa Canyon: any one of them would be worth going a long way to see. That you can take in all three in two or three days' walking is almost too good to be true.

The Cirque de Gavarnie is textbook geography, a classic glacial amphitheatre, but on a massive scale. Setting out on the easy track from Gavarnie village it doesn't look that far away, but it keeps on getting bigger. Most of the tourists opt to make the journey on mule-back, making the walk a rather pungent experience.

▽ *Upper reaches of the Cirque de Gavarnie, from les Entortes*

The mules don't go beyond the Holtellerie du Cirque; most of the people venture little further. Those who do either shout to raise echoes or, more likely, start talking in whispers. The walls seem to lean over you. The Grande Cascade spills in white streamers down almost 1,400 ft (422 m) of the left wall, while the tiered back walls are a winter Mecca for icefall climbers.

For mere walkers, it's hard to imagine that there's any way out, but there is a route, the Echelle des Sarradets, which finds a way up the wall opposite the Grande Cascade. And though 'Echelle' means ladder, it is mostly no more than steep walking, with a few short steps of moderate scrambling.

After 300 m (1,000 ft), the slope lies back, though the opposite wall of the Cirque still rises above you. Now an open valley and easy-angled rock ribs lead to the Refuge des Sarradets. Marmots bumble about, often foraging for scraps near the hut when the pickings are slim elsewhere. The hut terrace looks up to the Breche de Roland itself.

Legend relates that the hero Roland, fleeing his enemies, was trapped against the vertical walls that crest the ridge, but hewed the gap with one stroke of his sword Durandal. It's equally wondrous to contemplate two hanging glaciers, grinding away back-to-back until the rock between was worn down to the merest fin before being breached.

DESCRIPTION: 3 days' walking across rugged mountain terrain, staying in cosy refuges and mountain villages

LOCATION: the Pyrenees, on borders of France and Spain

WHEN TO GO: May to September, but the route is unlikely to be snow-free before August

START: Gavarnie, served by buses from Lourdes via Luz-Saint-Sauveur

FINISH: the route returns to Gavarnie

DURATION: typically 3 days, but there are many options for side trips (the ascent of Monte Perdido from Goriz hut is straightforward in late season when clear of snow)

MAX ALTITUDE: 2,805 m (9,203 ft) at Breche de Roland

ACCOMMODATION: two nights mountain huts, wider choice in Gavarnie and Torla

SPECIAL CONSIDERATIONS: in early season an ice-axe is essential and crampons may also be advisable

PERMITS/RESTRICTIONS: wild camping is restricted in the national parks on both sides of the border

GUIDEBOOK: *Walks and Climbs in the Pyrenees* by Kev Reynolds, pb Cicerone Press

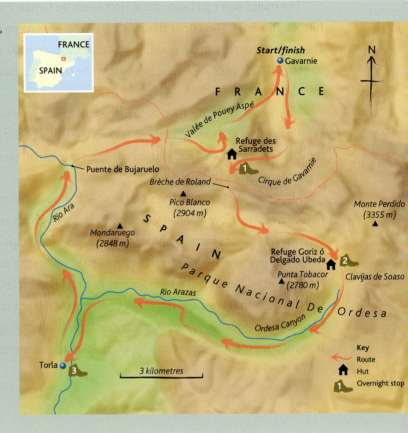

FRANCE
SPAIN

Start/finish
Gavarnie

F R A N C E

Valée de Pouey Aspé

Refuge des Sarradets

Puente de Bujaruelo

Brèche de Roland

Cirque de Gavarnie

Pico Blanco
(2904 m)

Monte Perdido
(3355 m)

Rio Ara

Mondaruego
(2848 m)

S P A I N

Refuge Goriz ó
Delgado Ubeda

Punta Tobacor
(2780 m)

Clavijas de Soaso

P a r q u e   N a c i o n a l   D e   O r d e s a

Rio Arazas

Rio Arazas

Ordesa Canyon

Torla

3 kilometres

Key
Route
Hut
Overnight stop

In the early season, the climb to the Breche will be over steep snow; later in the summer this generally disappears, leaving a more toilsome ascent over scree. The walls flanking the cleft are dead vertical, even overhanging in places, chopped off abruptly like battleship bows.

The Breche must be one of the world's great frontier crossings, too, though it's the change of landscape that you're aware of as you step into Spain; the southern side is drier and the sprawling slopes are pockmarked with hollows and sinkholes. The route to the Rifugio Goriz runs near the entrance to another extraordinary feature, the ice-filled Marboré caves, though these can't be explored without ropes, ice-axes and crampons.

Approaching Goriz, you begin to sense the world dropping away again. The full depth of the Ordesa canyon is only seen the following morning, as you descend into the mini-Gavarnie of the Circo de Soaso. The brave can go ape-fashion down hanging chains (Clavijas) but there's an easier, if more circuitous, alternative.

From Soaso you can hike steadily down the canyon floor, but the more inspiring route is the Faja de Pelay, a terrace path along the southern wall. It looks unlikely, but in reality holds few terrors, gliding through perched meadows and forest. The best bird's-eye views come at the end, at the Mirador de Calcilarruego, a stone balcony built out over a vertical prow.

From here cunning switchbacks descend 600 m (2,000 ft) to the valley floor, touching down close to the roadhead. A path, avoiding the road, wanders pleasantly past green pools and cascades to the compact stone village of Torla.

If you need to return to the French side, the most straightforward option is a steady ascent past the tiny hamlet of Bujaruelo to the frontier col (Puerto de Bujaruelo/Port de Boucharo). Start early as it's a longish day and the climb can get hot. Then follow the Haute Route de Pyrenees as if returning to the Refuge des Sarradets, before dropping down into the verdant Vallee de Pouey Aspe. The final steep descent back to Gavarnie gives more great views of the Cirque. Even now the mind still struggles to grasp the scale.

OVERLEAF *The Ordesa Canyon from the Faja de Pelay*

◁◁ *In the lower reaches of the Ordesa canyon, looking up to La Fraucata*

▽ *Clouds fill the Cirque de Gavarnie, from just below the Breche de Roland*

THE ALPS
Walkers' Haute Route

KEV REYNOLDS

▽ *Mont Blanc appears as a great block of snow and ice from the approach to Col de Balme*

The Pennine Alps contain the greatest collection of 4,000 m (13,123 ft) summits in western Europe, and to walk in their shadow from Mont Blanc to the Matterhorn is to unravel a chain of natural wonders. Day after day ice-fretted peaks form a backdrop, their crusted ridges pushing north to confuse the eastbound route. Valleys carved by long-vanished glaciers reward with flower meadows, lakes, boisterous streams and ribs of old moraine disguised by stands of larch or pine. Villages offer hotel comfort to the passing trekker, while a string of mountain huts provide a romantic style of lodging on the upper slopes.

◁ *On leaving the Sentier des Chamois a view opens across the deep basin of Lac de Louvie to the Combin massif on the far side of Val de Bagnes*

▽ *The Trient glacier is the main focus of attention on the steep haul to the Fenêtre d'Arpette.*

This is the Walkers' Haute Route, a strong contender for the title of Europe's Most Beautiful Trek.

It begins in Chamonix at the foot of Mont Blanc, but turns away from the icy monarch, and passing below a row of granite aiguilles dips in and out of forest on the way to Le Tour, the valley's highest village. Up a slope ablaze with scarlet alpenroses you gain the Col de Balme on the Franco/Swiss border, from which a retrospective view shows Mont Blanc framed by the Aiguilles Verte and Rouges. 'If that view does not thrill you,' wrote R.L.G. Irving in 1939, 'you are better away from the Alps.'

Nestling in its eponymous Swiss valley, Trient directs the next stage to Champex with two options. If conditions are bad, the lower route via the Bovine alp should be taken. But the alternative crossing of the 2,665 m (8,743 ft) Fenêtre d'Arpette is so good that it should be tackled if possible. Long, steep and scenic, it's a tough stage that forms the yardstick by which all subsequent passes will be measured.

From lakeside Champex to Le Châble in Val de Bagnes is a day's easy walking through a pastoral landscape. But the following stage is brutal by comparison, with over 1,600 m (5,250 ft) of ascent to reach Cabane du Mont Fort with its outlook dominated by the distant Mont Blanc range. If that were not enough, next morning takes you along a narrow terrace known as the Sentier des Chamois, which provides a chance to watch chamois and

▷▷ *The Matterhorn, that most iconic of mountains, above the Stellisee*

▽ *Having crossed the Augstbordpass, the route descends, then turns a spur to be confronted by the Dom, shining above the Ried glacier across the deep Mattertal*

ibex at close quarters, and has a breathtaking vista of the Combin massif – one of the glories of the Pennine Alps.

Three passes lead to Cabane de Prafleuri, above which Col des Roux looks out to Mont Blanc de Cheilon guarding the head of Val des Dix. Descending over boulders and through pastures shrill with the cry of marmots, the way continues along a track beside Lac des Dix, which forms part of the Grande Dixence hydro-electric scheme. At its far end you either take a direct path to Col de Riedmatten, or follow a moraine track to Cabane des Dix, then cross an easy glacier to the Pas de Chèvres.

The first is approached by a steep, gritty gully, while the lower crossing is noted for having three near-vertical ladders bolted to a steep rock face. The distant tip of the Matterhorn may be seen for the first time, but on the walk down to Arolla, Mont Collon is the dominant feature.

Three stages continue the Haute Route to Zinal via La Sage and Cabane de Moiry whose spectacular location has an icefall, glacier and horny crests of mountains nearby. On the third day Col de Sorebois leads to a knee-punishing descent into Zinal, backed by a host of majestic peaks.

DESCRIPTION: a challenging Alpine trek from Mont Blanc to the Matterhorn, with overnights in mountain huts or valley hotels

WHEN TO GO: July to September, but unseasonal snowfall can affect the route at any time

START: Chamonix (France), served by bus or train from Geneva

FINISH: Zermatt (Switzerland), with frequent trains to Geneva

DURATION: 14 days, but with options, including transport possibilities, to shorten the trek if needed

MAX ALTITUDE: 2,965 m (9,728 ft), Col de Prafleuri

ACCOMMODATION: mountain huts, with valley hotels and gîtes d'étape

LANGUAGES: French and German, although English is understood in most lodgings

SPECIAL CONSIDERATIONS: trekking poles advisable. In the early summer an ice axe could be useful

PERMITS/RESTRICTIONS: wild camping is forbidden in Switzerland

GUIDEBOOK: *Chamonix to Zermatt* by Kev Reynolds, pb Cicerone Press

The Turtmanntal is next, a peaceful backwater and a buffer of tranquillity on the way to the busy Mattertal, linked by the 2,894 m (9,495 ft) Augstbordpass — the final crossing and one of the best of the whole route. Below it you turn a spur to be greeted by the finest view too. Across the valley shines the Dom, highest mountain entirely in Switzerland; on the Mattertal's west flank the Weisshorn, while far away and closing the valley's head, a massive wall of snow and ice stretches from Liskam to Breithorn. It's a view guaranteed to stop you in your tracks.

On the long slog down to St Niklaus you squeeze between ancient hay barns and chalets in the prettiest hamlet in Switzerland, before tackling the two-day Europaweg, carved from the Mattertal's east flank. It's airy, in places scary, but a spectacular trek that brings you at last to the uplifting sight of the Matterhorn, the most iconic of Alpine peaks and a true natural wonder.

THE ITALIAN ALPS
The Sesto Dolomites

GILLIAN PRICE

Embedded in the Italian Alps, the Dolomites set themselves apart as a unique group of soaring jagged masses of pale sedimentary rock that have weathered into awe-inspiring sculptures. Variously likened to Egyptian obelisks, sharks' teeth and organ pipes, they are composed of dolomite, a rock akin to limestone but with the addition of magnesium; a discovery made by French geologist Déodat de Dolomieu, hence the name.

▽ *Walkers below Monte Paterno*

This walk explores the Sesto Dolomite group now in Italy's South Tyrol. This German-speaking region belonged to the Austrian-Hungarian Empire until the aftermath of the First World War. The hostilities saw the front line cut straight through these mountains and visitors encounter trenches and manmade rock tunnels everywhere, not to mention rusty barbed wire and even boot soles.

From the roadhead at Hotel Dolomitenhof, 1,454 m (4,771 ft) a lane leads through meadows bright with wildflowers and flanking the awesome Tre Scarperi massif. But you're more likely to be gazing straight ahead as a slice of the 'Sesto Sundial' comes into view due north: a semi-circle of impressive points corresponding to hours on a clock face: 10, 11, 12 and 1. After Rifugio Fondo Valle 1,548 m (5,079 ft) it's north up Alta Val Fiscalina. A steady climb ensues up the narrowing valley well above the tree line to the spectacularly-positioned Rifugio Zsigmondy-Comici at 2,224 m (7,297 ft). Keen eyes will make out the line of man-made caverns and ledges opposite on Monte Popera, marking the route of the wartime 'Strada degli Alpini', now a popular aided route.

▽ *The Tre Cime from Forcella Lavaredo*

Next you embark on a winding climb below towering Croda del Toni, following a military track to Passo Fiscalino, 2,519 m (8,265 ft). Scattered timbers and ruined trenchwork are poignant reminders of the fighting that took place here. Hardy alpine cinquefoil and bulbous gentians cling to the rock providing welcome splashes of colour. From the pass a broad ledge leads to cosy Rifugio Pian di Cengia, 2,528 m (8,294 ft), a haven from the often chilling winds.

Not far along is a notch in the rock crest, Forcella Pian di Cengia, 2,522 m (8,275 ft). This affords entry to a vast basin, almost eerie in its barrenness, soon belied as you pick up the scent of pink round-leaved penny cress and pretty yellow Rhaetian poppies that thrive on the blinding white scree. North-west high after a series of tarns is Rifugio Locatelli, 2,405 m (7,891 ft). What a spot! Perfectly positioned to catch the sun's setting colours on the magnificent Tre Cime formation to the south. This unrivalled trio, shaped by erosion along ancient fault lines, soars to 2,999 m (9,840 ft) on the central Cima Grande.

DESCRIPTION: a superb 3-day trek across the spectacular Sesto Dolomites, where every step comes complete with a breathtaking panorama

LOCATION: The Sesto Dolomites, in the north-east corner of the Italian Alps, near the border with Austria

WHEN TO GO: May to October; however the huts are open from mid-June to late September. In winter Val Fiscalina has a cross-country ski piste, and many valleys can be followed for snowshoe excursions

START: Hotel Dolomitenhof in Val Fiscalina. Summer bus service from San Candido in Val Pusteria and the closest railway station

FINISH: Landro, where a bus can be taken back to Val Pusteria

DURATION: 11 hrs + side trips = three days

MAX ALTITUDE: 2,539 m (8,330 ft) on Sasso di Sesto

ACCOMMODATION: mountain huts

SPECIAL CONSIDERATIONS : headlamp handy for exploring tunnels

PERMITS/RESTRICTIONS: wild camping is forbidden in the Sesto Dolomites as it is a nature park

GUIDEBOOKS: *Walking in the Dolomites* and *Shorter Walks in the Dolomites* by Gillian Price, pb Cicerone

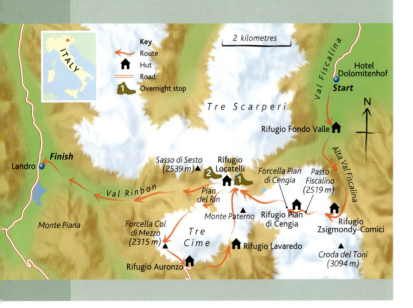

A good half day can fruitfully be spent in the proximity of Rifugio Locatelli exploring wartime tunnels. Scramble up to the narrow ridge and past the curious Frankfurter Wurstel rock sausage to find low tunnels hewn in the rock, threading their way through Monte Paterno.

A further rewarding side trip is to Sasso di Sesto at the rear of the hut; the flattish 2,539 m (8,330 ft) top has breathtaking views. Afterwards from the saddle veer left below Torre di Toblin to a 2,457 m (8,061 ft) pass, amidst abandoned wartime fortifications and vast trench systems. Complete the loop back to the hut.

Now for the spectacular four-hour circumnavigation of the Tre Cime. A good path traverses grassy Pian del Rin, home to burrowing marmots. Past an old shepherd's hut you climb to Forcella Col di Mezzo, 2,315 m (7,596 ft), the far western corner of the Tre Cime. The spectacular route continues to Rifugio Auronzo and its vast car park. While admiring the crazy profile of the Cadini range, take the lane coasting east via a chapel to Rifugio Lavaredo, and thence to Forcella Lavaredo, 2,454 m (8,052 ft). Here you enter the central amphitheatre once more. A narrow, exciting path hugging the eastern flank of Monte Paterno crosses to Rifugio Locatelli.

When you've had your fill of these magnificent surroundings, head west across the rock terraces. Down a forbidding rock barrier dwarf mountain pines accompany tight zigzags into Val Rinbon, with brilliant views of Croda Rossa ahead. Alpenrose shrubs and larch abound as you descend to meadows alongside Monte Piana, before the road at Landro, with concluding vistas of the Tre Cime.

△ *Traversing snow on Monte Paterno*

SICILY
Mt Etna

GILLIAN PRICE

△ *Cutting a path through volcanic ash, Valle del Bove*

Fire-breathing monster, forge of the Gods, bringer of destruction yet supreme provider of fertility, Mount Etna is not your run-of-the-mill volcano. Towering to 3,350 m (10991 ft) above sea level, Mongibello – 'mountain par excellence' according to its Arabic appellation – is the highest active volcano in Europe; a fact visitors will appreciate when landing at Catania airport, at the foot of this smoke-billowing giant. Starting with modest underwater eruptions, it has taken over three hundred thousand years for *'a muntagna* (as it is known to the Sicilians) to achieve this impressive height, while at the same time spreading over a base 160 km (100 miles) around, with memorable landscapes all the way.

Low on Etna's immense slopes, orchards of choice pistachios and grapes thrive. Higher up all appears barren, a chaos of rock and sand. However colonizing plants are ever active. Broom roots split stones, while miraculous cushions of milk vetch – aka 'holy thorn' (*spina santa*) – fix mobile sands. The record for hardiness goes to the endemic camomile and ragwort which flourish at 3,000 m (9,840 ft).

Full day walks are described on both the southern and northern flanks of Mount Etna. From Area Etna Sud, 1,900 m (6,234 ft) and landmark Rifugio Sapienza, survivor of decades of invasive lava and hot ash onslaughts, take the road east past the car parks. Minutes along are the long-extinct Monti Silvestri. These craters are among the three hundred so-called parasitic cones formed by lava seeping out along radial fault lines down Etna's flanks. Both upper (*superiori*) and lower (*inferiori*) mounts are worth exploring for their rainbow-coloured sands (1.5 hrs for a complete visit). Don't miss the volcanic bombs, gigantic cannonballs of solidified lava hurled out of the volcano and cooled, whirling, in flight.

Further along the road, a clear path climbs through pine wood and broom shrubs. Across masses of hardy cushion flowers and even violets, it emerges on the Schiena dell'Asino, a dizzy crest above spectacular Valle del Bove. 5 km (3.1 miles) wide, 8 km (4.9 miles) long, this yawning valley receives the bulk of the lava flows from the summit craters. The area is bare and wind-swept and yields stunning views to the Ionian coast. Head up the ridge past a plaque, then with special care ascend to the 2,300 m (7,546 ft) mark, below La Montagnola peak. Where faint paths appear point your boots downhill for a fun running descent south-west across the fine black sand. Detour to the rear of Monte Calcarazzi and join the 4WD track near the gondola car for the final stretch to Rifugio Sapienza (4 hrs in all).

On Etna's northern side, start from Rifugio Brunek, 1,400 m, (4,593 ft) on the forestry track (*pista*) girdling the volcano's midriff. Accompanied by vast views over the Sicilian interior with the Peloritani and the Nebrodi ranges, it's 7km (4.3 miles) in gentle ascent. En route are curious coils of ropey lava and awesome black lava carpets through pine

▽ *A river of lava flowing from Mount Etna*

▷▷ *The snowcapped peak of Mt Etna rises above orange groves*

woods, their silent trail of devastation punctuated by *dagala*, islands of bright green that escaped what Italian writer Carlo Levi called the 'black milk of Etna's breast'. From the 1,700 m (5,580 ft) mark climb a faint path to Grotta dei Lamponi, an amazing underground tube-like cave. Such tunnels are formed when the upper surface of a river of lava cools and solidifies, whilst the flow continues beneath, emptying out as an eruption ends. With care it is possible to walk the entire 1 km (0.62 mile) length of the cave to its upper exit. Return along the same track to Rifugio Brunek, allowing three and a half hours total.

A fatiguing optional extension leads to a higher cave, Grotta del Gelo at 2,030 m (6,660 ft), which hosts a unique fossil glacier, though visitor limits may apply.

facts and figures

DESCRIPTION: a series of exciting day walks across the awesome volcanic slopes of Mount Etna, a mere crow's flight from the glittering sea!

LOCATION: the north-eastern corner of Sicily, easily reached from Catania

WHEN TO GO: May to October. Otherwise increased chance of snow on the upper slopes

START/FINISH 1: Area Etna Sud, Rifugio Sapienza, served by daily coach from Catania

START/FINISH 2: Rifugio Brunek on the SP Mareneve road 15 km (9.3 miles) above Linguaglossa (train from Catania)

DURATION: 2 days

MAX ALTITUDE: 2,300 m (6,546 ft) on the Schiena dell'Asino

ACCOMMODATION: hotel standard Rifugio Sapienza or B&Bs at Nicolosi. Refuge-style lodgings on the northern side

SPECIAL CONSIDERATIONS: walking boots with tough soles are needed for the abrasive lava. Gaiters are handy for the fine volcanic sand. A torch is useful for the cave. Warm clothing is needed year-round as it can be cold at these altitudes even when sunny

PERMITS/RESTRICTIONS: due to volcanic activity, walkers must not proceed unaccompanied above 2,700 m (8858 ft). Poisonous gases are present and low cloud can be disorienting. Depending on conditions, qualified guides (www.etnaguide.com) take visitors to the summit craters. Access to Grotta del Gelo is sometimes restricted; check with Park Authorities

GUIDEBOOK: *Walking in Sicily* by Gillian Price (Cicerone)

ITALY

SICILY

5 kilometres

Grotta dei Lamponi

Rifugio Brunek
Start/finish

Grotta del Gelo

Mount Etna

Central crater

Key
Route
Hut
Road

Valle del Bove

La Montagnola (2644 m)▲

Schiena dell'Asino

N

Start/finish
Rifugio Sapienza

Monti Silvestri

PICOS DE EUROPA

JON SPARKS

▽ Naranjo de Bulnes from Collado Pandebano

The Picos de Europa were named by mariners, their knuckly ridges often being the first sight of Europe. The range itself is compact but complex; as their fierce appearance promises, many of the ridges demand serious scrambling, even roped climbing. Routes for pure walkers are often convoluted. The going is sometimes rough, water sources are limited, and deep gaps separate distinct massifs, so big ascents and descents are inescapable on some stages. However, these can be interspersed with easier days of high wandering.

◁ *Descending Pico Cotalba*

Starting from Sotres, 1,000m (3,300 ft) above the sea, gives a good leg-up. Dirt roads and a good path lead to the broad Collado Pandebano: ahead the ground falls again towards Bulnes, perched at the throat of a deepening gorge. Our way swings left: a long steady slanting climb. The improbable peak of El Naranjo de Bulnes shoulders into view. Paradoxically both lumpy and soaring, it dominates the final switchbacks into the stony hollow of Vega Urriellu. Its 500 m (1,650 ft) West Face seems to lean over the hut, glowing dusty orange in the evening sun.

Continue southward, skirting the deep pit of Jou sin Tierre. Freely translated, this means 'bottomless hole', alluding to dark mysterious fissures in the limestone. The Picos are as important for cavers as for climbers; some of the deepest cave systems in Europe lurk here.

Across a second hollow, then the path climbs steeply to a col, Horcados Rojos. The flanking peak, Torre de los Horcados Rojos, can be tacked on as a side trip. Dropping down from the col, you pass the bivouac shelter of Cabana Veronica, reputedly once part of an aircraft carrier, then swing westward. The route is complex and may encounter patches of old snow. A steep gully, with some moderate scrambling, leads down into Hoyo del Llambrion, from where a final short descent reaches the Refugio de Collado Jermoso on its airy perch.

This scrambling is unavoidable without making a very long detour. The simplest way is to swing left before Cabana Veronica and descend to El Cable, then make a long climb back up to Refugio de Collado Jermoso from Fuente De. This makes a monstrous day from Urriellu.

OVERLEAF *Eastern Massif*

55

DESCRIPTION: a week's walking across dry, rugged ranges, with some tough stages alternating with much easier days

LOCATION: the Picos de Europa, shared by the provinces of Asturias, Cantabria and Léon in northern Spain

WHEN TO GO: mid-June to late September. August is busy and has a higher risk of afternoon thunderstorms

START: Sotres, reached by bus or taxi from Arenas de Cabrales

FINISH: Puente Poncebos; return to Arenas by the same road

DURATION: 7 days, 6 nights

MAX ALTITUDE: approx 2,600 m (8,530 ft)

ACCOMMODATION: 4 nights mountain huts, 2 nights in villages

SPECIAL CONSIDERATIONS: a good level of fitness and a familiarity with rough ground are essential. There is some moderate scrambling, not easily avoided. It is important to carry enough water as springs are few and far between

PERMITS/RESTRICTIONS: wild camping is discouraged

GUIDEBOOK: *Walks and Climbs in the Picos de Europa* by Robin Walker pb Cicerone Press

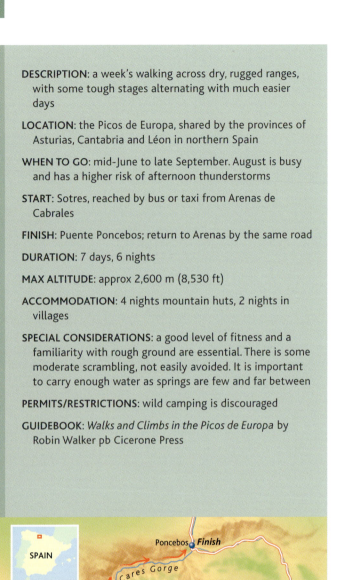

Alternatively, reach Cordinanes direct from Fuente De by valley paths or even by road.

From Collado Jermoso it's a long steep descent to Cordinanes, with spectacular sections of path traversing huge walls. Take time and enjoy it, because Cordinanes lies in the deep gash between central and western massifs, and the following day is a long one.

There's an easy opening across wooded slopes before swinging up into the great gully of Canal de Capozo. Steep switchbacks, then easier gradients, gain the greenery of Vega Huerta and the ruins of an old refuge. It's a fine lunch spot under the vast south face of Pena Santa de Castilla, the highest peak in the western massif.

△ *Refugio de Vegarredonda*

A fair path weaves its way to Jou las Pozas, but becomes vague as it traverses the slopes below La Torrezuela. Then it's plain sailing again to the Collado Les Merines, from where it's all downhill to the longed-for Refugio de Vegarredonda.

An easier day is now called for, and a wander to Mirador de Ordiales fits the bill perfectly. This is a fabulous balcony, perched above sheer cliffs, with far-reaching views of the Cordillera Cantabrica. It's easy to take in Pico de Cotalba, 2,026 m (6,647 ft) and adventurous scramblers can continue over the sharper ridge of El Requexon. Or simply meander back to Vegarredonda, taking time to discover the shy flowers that hide in limestone clefts.

It's possible to escape downhill from Vegarredonda to the tourist-thronged Lago Enol, but a fuller tour demands one last uphill effort, initially retracing a path already travelled, then forking left to grind up to Collado la Fragua. A snaking route eventually gains the great bowl of Jou Santu, traversing its north side on a sometimes sketchy path to the gash of El Boquete and a sudden view of the Central Massif. From here it's a 1,600 m (5,250 ft) descent to the village of Cain.

The last day is a complete – and now welcome – contrast, an easy downhill stroll on a broad path through the cool profundity of the Cares Gorge to Poncebos.

◁◁ *Looking up at El Naranjo de Bulnes, with the West Face in sunlight*

RODOPI MOUNTAINS

JON SPARKS

Bulgaria is one of the least known nations in today's Europe, yet as a new EU member is now readily accessible. Whatever the other consequences of its half-century of Communist rule, much of rural Bulgaria seems to have been locked in a virtual time-warp since before the Second World War. Its mountains in particular, outside a few modest ski resorts, boast some of the most pristine habitats on the continent.

The longest range, though not the highest, is the Rodopi (sometimes spelt Rhodope), which span around 225 km (140 miles) from east to west and nearly 100 km (62 miles) from north to south, where they sprawl across the border into Greece. The Rodopi peaks are relatively modest, reaching a maximum of 2,191m (7,189 ft) at Golyam Perelik. There are dramatic crags, gorges, caves and natural arches but what makes the Rodopi special is the unspoiled environment.

Here the rural way of life seems scarcely touched by the turbulence of the twentieth century. Wolves and brown bears roam the mountains, wild cats prowl in the deep forests and an amazing 37 species of raptor stalk the skies. Summers are long and sunny; meadows glow with flowers while the forest offers a welcoming coolness. This is a good place to walk alone, savouring one of the rarest, most precious qualities in today's world: silence.

Bulgaria is a cultural melting pot of Greek, Turkish and Slavic influences. The Greek influence is particularly strong in the Rodopi and the area claims to be the birthplace of the mythical hero Orpheus, whose lyre calmed birds and beasts, and made rocks and trees dance. The second peak of the range is named for him and some feel that his influence lingers in the tranquility of the mountains and the abundance of wildlife.

The modest scale of the mountains lends itself to day walking and it's easy to base yourself in a traditional village such as Yagodina and range out onto the surrounding ridges and valleys. A few short drives by bus or minibus extend the options further. Almost any walk here is a delight, but naturally there are highlights that should be on every visitor's agenda.

The geology of the Rodopis is complex but limestone dominates in the west, giving rise to deep gorges and a labyrinth of caves – over 150 are known. The Buynovsko Gorge, close to Yagodina, is the site of the Yagodinska Cave, noted for its flowstone formations as well as a 6,000-year old dwelling. A walk through the echoing shadows of the gorge can be combined with the high crest of the Sveti Iliya (Saint Elijah) ridge, which commands broad views over most of the western Rodopi range. It's a favoured area for spotting birds of prey.

Probably the grandest of the Rodopi gorges is the Trigrad Gorge, its walls rearing up to 250 m (820 ft) above the river. The main feature of the gorge is the gaping mouth of the

▽ *The remarkable rock arches of Chudnite Mostove (Wonderful Bridges)*

▷ *Honey Buzzard*

facts and figures

DESCRIPTION: straightforward day-walks from simple hotels and guesthouses in tranquil mountain surroundings

LOCATION: the Rodopi mountains, in southern Bulgaria

WHEN TO GO: May to October. The area is also ideal for snow-shoe tours in winter

BASE: the village of Yagodina, reached by road from Devin, 70 km (45 miles) from Bulgaria's second city, Plovdiv

DURATION: flexible; many operators offer one-week trips

MAX ALTITUDE: the highest peak is 2,191m (7,189 ft) but most walks stay lower

ACCOMMODATION: simple, comfortable hotels or guest-houses

SPECIAL CONSIDERATIONS/EQUIPMENT NEEDED: none

PERMITS/RESTRICTIONS: none

GUIDEBOOK: *The Rough Guide to Bulgaria* by Jonathan Bousfield & Dan Richardson, pb Rough Guides

BULGARIA

R o d o p i s

Yagodina

Buynovsko Gorge

Trigrad Gorge

Trigrad

Key
— Road
--- Walking routes

5 kilometres

Devil's Throat Cave, once believed to be an entrance to Hades; local legend maintains that Orpheus emerged here after descending into the underworld in attempt to recover his wife Eurydice. This suggests that hell is a colder place than generally imagined, as there's a permanent chill in the air around the entrance. Deep inside is a waterfall 42 m (138 ft) high, its ceaseless sound reverberating around the vast chamber and threatening to overwhelm the senses. The walls of the gorge are also a haunt of the rare wallcreeper, a striking bird with crimson wings; its name exactly describes its distinctive habits. Below the gorge is the village of Trigrad, where Christian and Muslim communities coexist in long-established harmony.

△*The rugged walls of the Trigrad Gorge*

The natural richness of the Rodopi is seen at its best on another circuit from Yagodina, climbing onto Mount Durdaga. The route transects old-growth forests, hung with lichens and home to wild boar and deer, as well as crossing luxuriant flower-meadows. The botanic feast continues on an old Roman road perched spectacularly above the Trigrad gorge, where the stunning views compete for attention with the wealth of flowers and butterflies.

Last but not least are the Chudnite Mostove, which translates as the Wonderful Bridges, a pair of remarkable rock arches, the larger 96 m (315 ft) in length. Lying close to the road, they are often visited on the journey into or out of the mountains.

DEVON AND DORSET
Jurassic Coast

RONALD TURNBULL

Britain claims to have more geology than any other country: not in area, obviously, but in variety. Britain's small but well-eroded hilltops show lots of rock; thousands of miles of Atlantic-battered sea cliff show even more. And Britain really does have a bit of everything. In the Western Isles is a fragment of earliest ancient continent; along the Scottish border, the remains of a continental collision. There are ancient volcanoes of the continental edge (Snowdonia, Lakeland) and of a rift valley (Edinburgh). The first four of the nine geological periods are named from bits of Britain – Cambria is Wales, and the Ordovices and Silures are early Welshmen. And the Jurassic could, but for a late attack of untypical UK modesty, have been the 'Dorsetian'.

▽ *Chalk cliffs of Swyre Head, east of Osmington*

Elsewhere in this book, eight days could give you an awful lot of volcanic lava (the Canaries) or of limestone (the Picos). Eight days of Devon and Dorset give you 150 million years of everything there is.

The 115 miles (180 km) of the Jurassic Coast form Britain's first natural World Heritage Site. The South-West Coast Path gives straightforward waymarked walking throughout, along paths established by the coastguard patrols 200 years ago; there are alternative paths, equally tempting, alongside. Walking eastwards usually means with the wind and rain at your back; it's also geologically upwards in time.

From Exmouth, the cliffs are reddish-brown: the red iron staining implies hot dry

desert. Cross-bedded dune sandstones can be seen around the base of Orcombe Point. This New Red Sandstone eroded out of a mountain range to the south, raised by the collision of Africa with the corner of Spain. At Budleigh Salterton are spectacular cliffs embedded with white quartzite, the pebbles washed out of those now non-existent mountains by powerful rivers flowing across country that is now the English Channel.

At Sidmouth the cliffs are stripy, topped off with greensand and then chalk. Between the stripes, 80 million years are missing: it's the Great Unconformity. But for geologists, the really exciting bit is around Lyme Regis. Here the entire Jurassic Period is displayed, with sea erosion constantly bringing fresh fossils down onto the beach to be found by serious professors and casual walkers alike. Here, 200 years ago, were discovered the plesiosaur and the ichthyosaur, sea-serpents and dino-sharks. Of the 74 ammonite bands identified within the Jurassic, 71 can be found at Lyme.

Four or five days (and about 100 million years) into the walk, Chesil Beach is a fascinating stretch of graded pebble shingle stretching for 28 km (17 miles). Pebbles aren't enough to keep me fascinated for 17 miles – so I suggest diverting inland here across the huge hill settlement of Maiden Castle to Dorchester, a handsome market town with useful shops and a railway station.

△ *Durdle Door. The bed of harder limestone has been raised upright by Alpine earth movements*

OVERLEAF *Lulworth Cove*

65

LOCATION: Devon and Dorset, southern UK

WHEN TO GO: year round, but best accommodation options and weather Easter to September

START: Exmouth, which has a railway station

FINISH: Poole, also with railway station

DURATION: 10–14 days, easily divided into shorter sections

MAX ALTITUDE: 191 m (626 ft) at Golden Cap

ACCOMMODATION: hotels, bed-and-breakfast, etc., at many points along or alongside the route

SPECIAL CONSIDERATIONS: bring a raincoat: it can rain at any time of the year

PERMITS/RESTRICTIONS: keep to rights-of-way, all of which are waymarked and are on Ordnance Survey maps; access through military ranges at Lulworth is restricted but paths are open most weekends and in high summer (see www.lulworth.com tel. +44 (0)1929 462721)

GUIDEBOOK: *The South West Coast Path* by Paddy Dillon, pb Cicerone; Ordnance Survey Explorer maps (1:25,000) 115, 116 and OL15

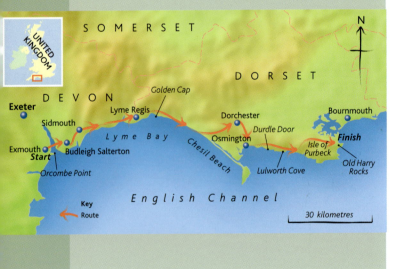

Gentle downland then leads southeast, by way of White Horse Hill. The white horse has been outlined on its south flank by removing turf to expose the chalk. You can rejoin the coast path at Osmington.

You could just enjoy the up-and-down swoop of the grassy clifftop path and ignore the still-fascinating rocks, now limestone underlying chalk. But offshore are small stacks of a tougher sort of limestone; and at Durdle Door you realize that this harder stratum has been lifted upright and then pierced by the sea, forming a spectacular arch. Another bout of distant mountain-building, the rise of the Alps, did the lifting.

And just as you think you're suffering terminal geology fatigue, along comes the fossil forest; stumps of ancient cypress and giant ferns, swamped by a shallow lagoon that encrusted it all with limestone.

The Coast Path continues above Dancing Ledge, where two-metre wide ammonites, *Titanites*, lie on the wave-swept ledges of Portland Stone beloved by scuba divers. But I prefer the higher path, along the Purbeck Ridge, to enjoy the downland butterflies and flowers. The ridge is the same hard limestone that formed the Durdle Door: but eventually it dips to the coast once again. At Old Harry Rocks, the chalk confronts the sea – but the sea's winning! Impressive arches and stacks make an appropriate end to a walk of cliff-edge thrills, good paths, and near-compulsion to study (did you think it was boring?) the science of the rocks.

▷ *Bindon Hill. The coast path demands frequent climbs and descents*

CANARY ISLANDS
Tenerife and La Gomera

RONALD TURNBULL

In 1492, as Christopher Columbus sailed past, Tenerife was inhabited by neolithic tribesmen and its volcano, El Teide, was in the midst of an eruption. Columbus, when he arrived at the other side, never did work out what continent he'd got to – and the same is true of Tenerife. The Canary Islands may rise alongside Saharan Africa, but politically they're part of the European Union; and historically, they're half way to South America.

But their rocks, and the forests and strange scrubby plants that cover them, don't belong to any continent at all. Those rocks are volcanic basalt, from half way down to the centre of the earth, far, far below the plate tectonic processes that produce continental drift. Such hot-spots are still a mystery to Earth scientists.

▽ *New and Old World plants grow together at El Botanico garden, Puerto Cruz*

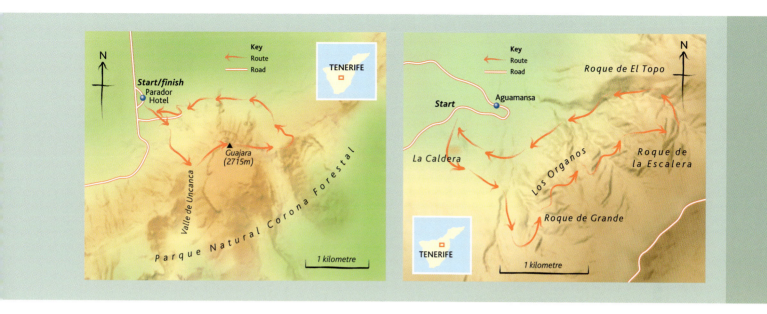

The cool Canarian current and north-east trade winds create a warm temperate climate quite unlike neighbouring Africa. The 3,500 m (10,000 ft) height of Tenerife meant that the ecology could adapt to ice ages and droughts by moving up or down the slope. The result is that the Canaries have over a hundred unique species: these include the mauve spires of the *tajinaste*, and the ancient brush-like dragon tree. They also have one unique ecosystem, the gloomy and haunting laurel forest, moistened by the clouds on the windward side-slopes.

All this is extremely accessible. The beach metropolis of Tenerife's southern corner means that cheap air flights arrive almost hourly. But the crowds are as easily escaped on local buses and inter-island ferries. The four walks are selected out of many to cover all four ecosystems. They are based at Puerto Cruz, on the fertile northern side of Tenerife; and at Valle Gran Rey on La Gomera, a ferry-ride and an island away to the south-west.

▽ *Canarian pine in cloud forest below Los Organos*

Tenerife: Los Organos

From the arid scrubland and palm trees of the coast, a half-hour bus ride from Puerto Cruz takes you up into forests of Canarian pine. Alight at La Caldera for the five-hour walk. Los Organos (the 'organ-pipes') is a steep cliff of basalt that has cooled into columns. Good forest paths lead up to, and then across, the crag face. The clouds that bathe this northern slope mean that the stunning ocean view is usually invisible, but there are plenty of succulent cactus-like cliff plants, and dramatic rock formations looming out of the mist. The return route, below the crag, is through open forest of tall Canarian pines.

▷▷ Tajinaste *(Echium wildpretii) grows only in the volcanic lava-fields of Tenerife*

Tenerife: Guajara

A volcanic crater is the top of the magma shaft that creates a single volcano; as seen on Kilimanjaro, or Vesuvius. Quite different is the volcanic caldera. As the magma chamber under a volcano empties, much of the country around can collapse, to make a hollow many kilometres wide.

El Teide may be the high point of Spain, but is a heap of volcanic rubble, with a funicular most of the way up. Far more worthwhile is neighbouring Guajara, on the caldera rim. This walk is short enough to allow a day-trip using the bus out of Puerto Cruz. Stay aboard up through the clouded forest zone, into a world of bright sunshine and bare, red-orange rocks. Start from the Parador Hotel.

The path winds up through cactus and the purple spikes of the *tajinaste*, onto a high shoulder of the mountain. A crag blocks the way, but the path takes to a shelf on the left hand side, with a view straight across to El Teide. A little scrambling is required, before the slope eases to the bare summit.

The descent is twisted rock-towers to the caldera floor. A smooth track takes you back through lava fields.

▽ *El Teide, the high point of Spain, seen from Guajara on the caldera rim*

LOCATION: Tenerife and La Gomera, Canary Islands

WHEN TO GO: year round, though snow is possible in winter on Guajara

START: Puerto Cruz, Tenerife

FINISH: Valle Gran Rey, La Gomera

DURATION: 4 days (but add beach time and more walks!)

MAX ALTITUDE: 2,715 m (8,800 ft) Guajara

ACCOMMODATION: hotels and apartments in Puerto Cruz and Valle Gran Rey

SPECIAL CONSIDERATIONS/EQUIPMENT NEEDED: none

PERMITS/RESTRICTIONS: El Teide, not included, requires a permit collected in person from Office of the National Park C/Emilio Calzadilla, n° 5 Santa Cruz de Tenerife

GUIDEBOOKS: *Walking in the Canary Islands: 1 West* by Paddy Dillon, pb Cicerone – apart from the Los Organos walk, in *Rough Guide to Tenerife and La Gomera* by Christian Williams, pb Rough Guides

La Gomera: Garajonay

Take an early-morning bus to Chipude. Good paths lead first to the rock-tower of La Fortaleza, whose summit requires a brief scramble. The continuing path to Garajonay takes you through a zone of giant tree heather. Then you plunge into laurel forest, deeply green and gloomy, to La Laguna Grande. Once back at Chipude, you can descend a steep and in places rather crumbled old path back to Valle Gran Rey.

La Gomera: Argaga gorge

This spectacular ravine runs up from the coast immediately south of Vueltas, into the basalt heart of the island. There is a lot of scrambling, not particularly technical, with the way marked with red paint spots and cairns. Eventually you'll emerge, 800m (2,700ft) above, at the white-painted Eremita de Nostra Senora de Guadaloupe. A path descends fairly comfortably and with great views to Valle Gran Rey.

AFRICA

"Africa is the Luminous Continent."

BOB GELDOF

△ *View of Giants Castle from Giants Cup, Drakensberg Mountains, South Africa*

Africa is vast; the second largest of the seven continents, after Asia. Its true size is understated on many maps, as the time-worn Mercator projection exaggerates areas in higher latitudes.

Africa's geography is not dominated by great linear mountain ranges, like the Alps, Andes and Himalaya, thrown up by continents in collision. Its greatest tectonic feature is the East African Rift System, where tectonic plates are tearing apart. Sometimes more accurately called the Afro-Arabian Rift, this extends from Jordan, where it forms the lowest point on the Earth's land surface at the Dead Sea, to Mozambique, a distance of over 6,400 km (4,000 miles). The second dominant feature is the Sahara, the world's largest desert.

Of course Africa does have mountains, with several ranges rising above 4,000 m (13,125 ft). The highest peaks are in East Africa; early European explorers were confounded by the appearance of white-capped mountains and it took some decades for the existence of 'Snow on the Equator' to be generally accepted. In fact Kilimanjaro, Mt Kenya and the Rwenzori range all have not just snow but glaciers, albeit small and probably diminishing. Kilimanjaro is not just the highest mountain in Africa but one of the world's great peaks, monumental in its isolation. At nearly 6,000 m (20,000 ft), it is the highest summit readily attainable by a non-mountaineer. It is the toughest challenge in this book and many fail to reach the top. For those who do, the sense of achievement is great, yet often overwhelmed by the astonishing glacial sculpture of the crater and the immense views.

Ethiopia's Simien range are a milder proposition, without permanent snow, but still reach over 4,500 m (14,800 ft), quite high enough to cause distress in those who are unfit or fail to acclimatize. Though the walking is relatively easy the plateau is violently terminated by huge precipices and dissected by deep gorges, giving breath-taking views. Unlike Kilimanjaro, the Simien are a fairly new destination and visitor numbers are still low. The local Amhara people greet visitors with a friendly curiosity born of unfamiliarity.

The Drakensberg mountains in southern Africa are the continent's spikiest range, spearing up savagely from the foothills and lending drama to an easy trek which crosses game-rich savanna and climbs onto rocky ridges.

Much smaller, and generally cooler, than the Sahara, the Namib Desert may be the world's oldest. Its stillness and emptiness are deceptive; a gentle trek brings insight into an otherwise unsuspected range of wildlife.

Inescapably, this is the poorest continent on Earth. Nowhere has more to gain from tourism, especially the right kind of tourism. But maybe, in the end, it's the visitor who gains most from exposure to Africa's extraordinary landscapes and its indomitable people.

OVERLEAF *Barrren vegetation and sand dunes typify the Namib Desert*

▽ *View of Drakensberg at Giants Castle*

DRAKENSBERG MOUNTAINS
Giant's Cup Hiking Trail

JON SPARKS

*S*traddling the border of South Africa and Lesotho, the Drakensberg (Dragon Mountain) range stretches nearly 200 km (125 miles) reaching its highest point – also the highest in southern Africa – at 3,482 m (11,424 ft) on Thabana Ntlenyana in Lesotho (a tough day walk from the dirt road at Sani Top). Sometimes likened to a thicket of spears, many of the peaks are wildly precipitous.

▽ *Crane Tarn*

The range is a hiker's paradise, but its steep rocky terrain means that many routes
entail serious scrambling. Organised campsites or huts are thin on the ground in the higher
areas and those planning longer hikes need to be self-sufficient, though it's often possible
to forego a tent as the area is well-provided with caves. These provide good shelter, though
you may need to chase out the baboons first!

△ *Rhino Peak*

A rare exception, and therefore the best introduction to the Drakensberg, is the five-
day Giant's Cup Hiking Trail. There are huts at each overnight stop, though you'll still need
to carry a stove, food and a sleeping bag. However, daily distances are modest and there
are many temptations to dawdle, soaking up the spectacular scenery and wildlife, or just
soaking in some of the fabulous rock pools. Alternatively, intriguing side-trips are possible
from the huts, with the advantage of being able to leave overnight gear behind. The terrain
is mostly open, grassy veld, which grows lush in the warm, moist summers. Eland and
several other species of antelope may be seen.

A gentle start from the foot of the Sani Pass sees the trail climb and then descend into the
Gxalingena valley to Ngenwa Pool. It may be hard to tear yourself away from this peaceful
place, especially as you face a more determined climb before descending to the Trout Beck. The
Trout Beck route can be difficult in wet weather so there's an alternative via Bypass Ridge. The
beck leads into the Pholela valley, with good views of the Giant's Cup itself – its profile making

the name self-explanatory – and on to the first night's stop at Pholela Hut, a lovely former farmhouse.

The second day is very short at just 9 km (5.6 miles), but this leaves plenty of time to admire the Tortoise Rocks and the San ('Bushman') paintings in Bathplug Cave. There are hundreds of cave art sites in the Drakensberg, but this is among the most notable, with hordes of small figures adorning the walls. Look, but don't touch. The cave is also a curious natural formation; at times a waterfall pours over the lip and seemingly disappears down a natural drain-hole, giving it its name. The trail soon descends Sipongweni Ridge to the thatched Mzimkulwana Hut, near which is a fine waterfall dropping into a deep pool.

Day three starts with a moderate climb onto Little Bamboo Mountain, named after the indigenous berg bamboo, and tops out at Crane Tarn, a gorgeous blue pool

DESCRIPTION: 5 days' hut-to-hut trek with moderate walking across grassy veld and over rocky ridges

LOCATION: uKhahlamba-Drakensberg Park, KwaZulu Natal, South Africa

WHEN TO GO: year-round. Snow possible in winter, thunderstorms in summer. Spring and autumn are best

START: road below Sani Pass

FINISH: Bushman's Nek

DURATION: typically 5 days, possible in less, but with many options for side trips

MAX ALTITUDE: approx 2,100 m (6,890 ft)

ACCOMMODATION: 4–5 nights in wilderness huts with bunks, mattresses, toilets

SPECIAL CONSIDERATIONS: sleeping bag, stove, food

PERMITS/RESTRICTIONS: permits needed from KwaZulu Natal Wildlife, hut space must be booked in advance; no wild camping or fires

GUIDEBOOK: *Hiking Trails of Southern Africa* by Willie and Sandra Olivier, Menasha Ridge Press

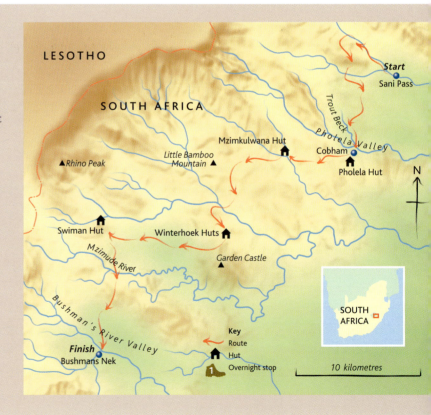

LESOTHO

SOUTH AFRICA

▲ Rhino Peak

Little Bamboo Mountain ▲

Mzimkulwana Hut

Cobham

Pholela Hut

Start
Sani Pass

Trout Beck

Pholela Valley

Swiman Hut

Winterhoek Huts

Mzimude River

Garden Castle ▲

Bushman's River Valley

Finish
Bushmans Nek

Key
Route
Hut
Overnight stop

N

SOUTH AFRICA

10 kilometres

fringed by golden grass. A little further on, scattered rocks turn out on closer inspection to be petrified trees.

△ Winterhoek Huts

The great mass of Garden Castle, one of the most striking peaks in the Drakensberg, now looms ahead as the trail heads, generally descending, towards the thatched rondavel-style Winterhoek Huts. In 1835, one of the first white explorers of the region, Captain Allen Gardiner, gave the peak its earlier name of Giant's Castle, recording that from certain angles it bore an uncanny resemblance to Edinburgh Castle. (Today a different peak bears the name Giant's Castle).

Day four opens with the steep climb to Black Eagle Pass, on the north side of Garden Castle. The effort is richly rewarded as the trail stays high, around the 2,000 m (6,565 ft) contour, for the next 6 km or so, with magnificent views. The spectacular scenery continues as the trail descends towards Swiman Hut, but pride of place undoubtedly goes to Rhino Peak, 3,051 m (10,007 ft); its likeness to a rhino's horn is unmistakable.

At the start of day five it's necessary to retrace your steps for about 1.5 km (1 mile), but in these surroundings that's no real hardship. After crossing the Mzimude River there's a steady climb to Langalibalele Cave on the flanks of the peak of the same name. The trail then winds down into Bushman's River Valley. The Bushman's Nek Hut lies near the end of the descent and from here it's a couple of miles to the end of the trail.

◁◁ Eland, Drakensburg Mountains

TANZANIA
Climbing Kilimanjaro

JON SPARKS

△ *Zebra graze with Mount Kilimanjaro looming in the distance*

YYou've heard of the Seven Summits, of course; the highest peaks of the seven continents. Kilimanjaro, Africa's highest point, stands fourth on this list. It is also widely held to be the world's highest free-standing mountain, rising over 4,000 m (13,000 ft) from the surrounding plains. Visible from afar, the snowy upper reaches seem to float above the heat-haze of the plains, detached from the earth.

Kilimanjaro is probably the highest summit that can be reached by a non-mountaineer. It is nonetheless a tough challenge, principally because the air at the summit is less than half as dense as at sea level. The chances of success, and of escaping the potentially fatal effects of Acute Mountain Sickness (AMS), are greatly improved by prior acclimatization. An ideal preparation is climbing Mount Meru, 4,566 m (14,981 ft) first; many tour operators offer combined trips to the two peaks.

Of half a dozen recognised routes, connoisseurs recommend the Rongai, the only one to approach the mountain from the north. This flank is much drier and the early stages cross archetypal African savannah. This is elephant country, though footprints and large piles of dung (impressive in themselves) may be all that you see. The first campsite is at the first Rongai Cave at 2,600 m (8,530 ft).

The second day is a steady ascent of about 1,000 m (3,300 ft) across heathery moorland, with the main peak, Kibo, and its satellite, Mawenzi, drawing ever nearer. At the second Rongai Cave, some walkers head directly towards Kibo, but the prudent bear left towards Mawenzi, to camp by the Kikelewa Caves at 3,600 m (11,810 ft).

The third day is relatively short but grows steeper, arriving at the lovely Mawenzi Tarn under the jagged outline of Mawenzi. Unlike Kibo, 5,149 m (16,894 ft) Mawenzi offers no easy route, and is climbed far less often, but it's an impressive backdrop to a camp on the shores of the tarn at 4,330 m (14,210 ft). A sensible schedule allows two nights at this beautiful, rarely crowded spot, exploring or just relaxing. It's at an ideal height for acclimatization.

Though the next day is not intrinsically hard, it's prudent to start early. It's a steady plod across the broad, bleak plateau of The Saddle towards massively looming Kibo. Finally the path converges with the other main routes. 'School Camp', at 4,750 m (15,585 ft) is an alternative to the crowded huts. Spend the afternoon resting, eating and drinking; early to bed, though whether you'll sleep is another question...

If you have slept, there's a rude awakening around midnight. Silvery moonlight or bobbing yellow pools of torchlight; bitter cold; the mountain a huge shadowy presence. The path is steep, winding, sometimes rocky. Find your own rhythm; those who start too fast

OVERLEAF *Summit glacier, Kilimanjaro*

▽ *Giant Groundsel (Senecio keniodendron) plants with Mawenzi in the distance, as seen from Horombo Hut*

usually pay for it later. Some bless their iPods, others focus on the sounds of the mountain; the slow crunching of boots, the thin fluting of the wind. The path steepens after the halfway point at Hans Meyer Cave, and now there may be snow underfoot, but the sky is paling in the east. Plod on, trying to draw energy from the growing light.

Reaching the crater rim, there's one last short push to Gillman's Point, 5,735 m (18,817 ft), ideally before the sun finally bursts over the horizon. Many of the

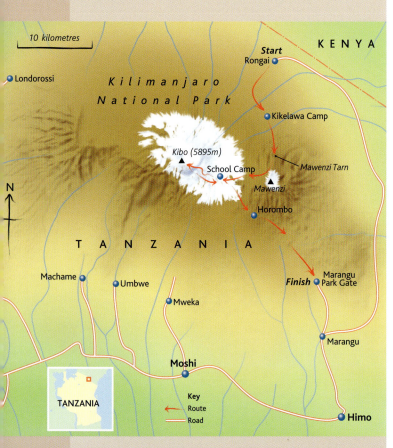

tourists get no further, but the worst is over. From here to the top is about 800 m (0.5 miles), over a couple of intervening bumps. Below, the light slowly creeps down the mountain to the slumbering plains.

The early light also delineates the strange pinnacles and flutings of the summit glaciers. These have retreated markedly in the past fifty years, though claims that they could vanish entirely in the next decade or two are disputed. At last, perhaps six hours after setting out, you reach Uhuru Point, the roof of Africa, and the widest view most of us will ever see.

Time on the summit is intense and usually brief; schedules typically dictate a long descent to Horombo, 3,720 m (12,205 ft), for the last night on the mountain, and then on down through misty rain-forest to Marangu.

▽ *The view of Mawenzi peak from Mawenzi Tarn*

NAMIBIA
The Namib Desert

ROGER BRAY

▽ *Bush showers, Tok Tokkie Trails camp*

For a few minutes as the sun rises or sets the dunes of the Namib desert are at their most theatrical. The rust red sand is rippled with shadow. Soft light produces distant graduations of grey and pink. Sparse yellow grass appears green, like a mirage. You rouse yourself in the chilly dawn or shake off weariness after a long hike to find the best vantage points, taking pictures furiously before the effect is lost in the blaze of day or sudden nightfall.

OVERLEAF *Sossusvlei Dunes*

The Namib is believed to be the world's oldest desert. It has existed for at least 55 million years. Driven by southerly winds, its dunes drift ceaselessly northward. The most spectacular are at Sossusvlei, though you are likely to have plenty of other day visitors for company.

For a real sense of the desert's astonishing ecology and the drama of its changing light and temperatures you should spend longer than a day on foot, sleeping under the dazzling southern stars. The place to do that is further south, in the NamibRand Nature Reserve.

Before striking out into this vast private reserve, half the size of Belgium, certain warnings must be heeded. Shake out your boots in the morning, lest a scorpion should have crept in. Avoid walking in single file since, unlike other snakes, the puff adder does not make off when it senses heavy footsteps, preferring to wait and weigh its options. By the time the third hiker approaches it feels threatened enough to strike. Its bite is not usually lethal but requires urgent medical attention.

We did not see a scorpion, though they are devilishly cunning, burrowing under the sand in spirals to fool predators like the bat-eared fox, which spits out their poisonous tails before devouring them. And the only puff adder we saw was coiled harmlessly in a pit at the farmhouse headquarters of Tok Tokkie Trails, a small, eco-sensitive outfit which provides guides and runs fixed overnight camps. Tok Tokkie is the name for various tenebrionid or surface beetles, derived from the tapping of their tails on the ground during courtship.

You might think creatures have a hard enough time surviving in arid surroundings without bothering about such rituals. Indeed, without expert instruction you might imagine very little exists there. As we walked to the first camp our guide quickly dispelled any such preconceptions. Here was the trace of the golden mole which "swims" just beneath the surface of the sand, there the prints of Ludwig's bustard. Occasionally, in the distance, we sighted springbok – and oryx, whose propensity to feed in the shade of a tree once enabled San bushmen to tell, from the position of the sun and the age of their droppings, when they were there and how far they might have wandered.

After dinner we retired to sleeping bags on camp beds spaced between low dunes, the cold night air noisy with the cries of barking geckos. As we breakfasted next morning a dune lark, endemic to the desert, came looking for crumbs.

We departed early, for even in early summer the midday heat is fierce. The route climbed gently over a low mountain pass, where bloodstains on rocks suggested a leopard kill, and across a stony plain where, incredibly, sheep were once farmed. We were introduced to more of the desert's resourceful residents, such as the fog-basking beetle which does a kind of hand stand when night mist rolls in from the ocean: moisture condenses on its back and trickles down into its mouth. We picnicked under a sunshade

▽ *Dead tree and dunes,*
Namib Desert

beneath a camel thorn tree. We had been advised to bring reading-matter for this siesta but our attention was diverted by pygmy falcons, returning to a nest of sociable weaver birds where, rather like cuckoos, they had taken lodgings.

Afternoon saw us slogging across dunes. The entire route covers only around 22 km (just under 14 miles) but when walking on sand, particularly when it has been heated by sun, distance is irrelevant. Guides move at the pace of the slowest and there are frequent pauses to study tracks or take in views. By the time we reached our second camp we had been on our feet for eight hours, and climbing the last few dunes was tiring.

On the final morning we were filled less with regret that the walk was done, more with a feeling of privilege at gaining so many insights into a world which had initially appeared impenetrable.

LOCATION: the NamibRand Nature Reserve, south-west Namibia

WHEN TO GO: guided walks are available from March 1 – November 30. May and September are good months

START/FINISH: Tok Tokkie Homestead, then by vehicle to start of walk

DURATION: afternoon, one full day and one morning. Longer itineraries are also available

MAX ALTITUDE: mostly around sea level

ACCOMMODATION: fixed camps with bucket showers, long drop toilets

SPECIAL CONSIDERATIONS: a reasonable level of fitness. High factor sunscreen, hat, glasses rather than contact lenses (sand can cause irritation), thermal underwear, sweater recommended for cold evenings (anything not wanted on the walk is transported to camps)

PERMITS/RESTRICTIONS: none

GUIDEBOOK: *Namibia* by Chris McIntyre, pb Bradt Travel Guides

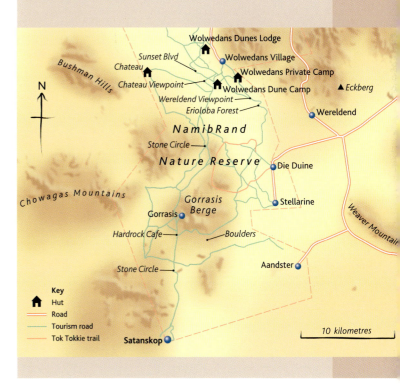

ETHIOPIA
The Simien Mountains

JON SPARKS

▷▷ *The view from Geech Camp*

▽ *Gelada baboon*

Ethiopia's Simien mountains take the form of a vast plateau, typically sloping away gently to south and east but cut off sharply to north and west where a ragged escarpment plunges away, rent by deep gorges. The starkly dramatic landscape is littered with abrupt pinnacles and towers of solidified magma marking the necks of ancient volcanoes. In 1925 Rosita Forbes saw it this way: 'A thousand years ago, when the old gods reigned in Ethiopia, they must have played chess with those stupendous crags.'

The gentle slopes of the plateau give mostly easy walking, but the great escarpment provides near-endless views. It's also a rich area for wildlife, though recent declines in the numbers of some species mean that it's on the World Heritage Endangered List. One must hope that a more peaceful political situation and the economic input from a growing number of visitors, trekkers included, will provide the background to better protect this magnificent, magical area.

One species that's almost certain to be encountered is the gelada baboon, unique to Ethiopia. It's not a true baboon but the sole surviving member of a distinct family of primates. It lives in large groups and the males, around twice the size of the females, have impressive golden-brown manes. Geladas are shy, fleeing readily onto vertical cliffs where few predators can follow. Unlike some baboons, they pose little threat to humans.

DESCRIPTION: sustained but not difficult trekking across high mountain plateau and ridges, with optional ascent of high peak(s)

LOCATION: Simien Mountains National Park in Gondar region, northern Ethiopia

WHEN TO GO: October to early March is the dry season

START: Debark, reached by road from Gondar

FINISH: Adi Arkai, road link to Gondar

DURATION: 9–10 days trekking

MAX ALTITUDE: 4,533 m (14,873 ft) on peak, around 4,000 m (13,125 ft) on trek

ACCOMMODATION: camping, with all gear normally carried by mule

SPECIAL CONSIDERATIONS/EQUIPMENT NEEDED: be prepared for high altitude

PERMITS/RESTRICTIONS: none

GUIDEBOOK: *Ethiopia & Eritrea* by Matt Phillips, pb Lonely Planet

ETHIOPIA

N

Key
Route
Road

Finish — Adi Arkai
Sona
Imet Gogo
Geech Abyss
Geech — Chnneck
Ambiko
Ras Dashen
Sankabar
10 kilometres
Start — Debark

A variety of raptors ride the updraughts along the cliffs, the most spectacular being the lammergeiers with their three-metre wingspans. There's something almost prehistoric about these huge birds, strengthening the sense, common in the Simien, of being in a lost world.

There's a fairly standard trekking route across the plateau which includes the chance to reach the summit of Ethiopia's highest peak, as well as several others. The walking is generally straightforward but the high altitude – mostly between 3,500 and 4,000 m (11,485 – 13,125 ft) – can pose problems for some, especially those who try to rush, rather than taking time to acclimatize.

The starting point is the small town of Debark (sometimes spelt Debareq), where independent travellers should have little difficulty arranging guides and mules to carry baggage. Some drive from here to Sankabar, others begin the trek from Debark itself, which aids acclimatization.

It's a longish day from Sankabar to Geech, but along the way there are extraordinary views of the gorge known as the Geech abyss. In the immediate aftermath of the rainy season there's a spectacular waterfall plunging over 500 m (1,640 ft). Camp is near the Amhara village of Geech at an altitude of about 3,600 m (11,812 ft).

A common stratagem is to stay two nights at Geech, using the day to hike up to Imet Gogo, 3,926 m (12,881 ft), poised at the end of a ridge thrust out from the escarpment with vast drops on three sides. It's also a good place to look ahead to the higher peaks of the range.

Moving on from Geech the route continues mostly along the edge of the escarpment, breasting the 4,000 m (13,125 ft) contour for the first time and over

4,070 m (13, 354 ft) Inatye before descending to camp at Chennek almost surrounded by cliffs. Another fairly long day offers good prospects of sighting the Walia Ibex, a rare species now found only in these mountains, on the way to Ambiko (also spelt Ambiquo).

Ambiko is the base for the ascent of Ras Dejen (also spelt Dashen). Its true altitude is around 4,533 m (14,873 ft) though this is often claimed to be higher. It's undisputedly the highest peak in Ethiopia and is often stated also to be the fourth highest in all Africa, though it's more accurate to say that this is the fourth highest massif. A dawn start is customary and the temperature may be below freezing, but the climb is not difficult. Much of the way lies through weird forests of giant lobelia before emerging onto bare ridges where a short scramble gains the summit and an awesome panorama which, on a clear day, stretches into Eritrea.

From Ambiko an undulating route through mostly cultivated country leads to another camp on the plateau edge at Sona. From here there's a long descent into the Ansiya valley and even the chance of a swim. The change of scene into the lowlands brings lusher surroundings and a different perspective on the highlands you've left behind. From here there's a choice of routes to the road at Adi Arkai and the long bus trip back to Gondar.

▽ *Giant lobelia on Imet Gogo*

ASIA

"I have not told half of what I saw."

MARCO POLO

△ *Asia is home to the world's highest peaks*

Strictly speaking, according to the geographers, we should speak of Eurasia. The dividing line between Europe and Asia is mere convention, with no basis in physical geography. But even if we accept this division, Asia is too immense, and too diverse, to readily comprehend. Bigger than North and South America combined, Asia has around 60% of the entire human population, yet is home to the world's most thinly populated nation.

The Asian mainland alone, not counting islands, stretches from just north of the Equator far into the Arctic. West to east it spans more than a third of the way round the globe. It has the greatest diversity of environments and habitats on the planet; it has all of the world's mountains over 7,000 m (22,966 ft), the world's deepest and oldest lake, the wettest place on earth, and the coldest outside Antarctica.

To try and grasp any of this immensity by walking might seem impossible, yet how else could you do it? The four routes featured here are hugely different, geographically and culturally, yet barely begin to scratch the surface.

The world's highest mountain is a magnetic attraction. By the time this book appears the number of people to have climbed Mt Everest will have passed 2000. Every year, thousands more trek to a point where they can see it. Yet if those minutes – or, at best, hours – gazing on the peak are the goal, it's often the journey that provides the most enduring memories. It is not just a trek through the greatest mountains on earth, but through the homeland of its greatest mountaineers, the Sherpa people.

If the Himalaya impress with vertical immensity, it's the immensity of horizontal distance that impinges in Mongolia, an almost empty land where high plains of golden grass stretch far beyond the horizon. Yet perhaps the best way to experience this limitless space is on horseback or – an increasingly popular choice – by bicycle. For walkers the distances are almost too daunting. In the far west the steppes rumple up into mountains; a trek here has variety, and that simple sense of having somewhere to aim for.

From the landlocked emptiness of Mongolia to steamy, bustling Malaysia is a leap that exemplifies Asia's contrasts. Here Mt Kinabalu's granite spires rise starkly from the tropical forests. The thin air and the chill of a pre-dawn summit ascent catch many unawares, but for those who prepare sensibly the ascent is not unduly arduous. Kinabalu invites comparisons with Africa's Kilimanjaro, despite being almost 2,000 m (6,500 ft) lower. Both are isolated mountains, far higher than anything else in sight. This lordly pre-eminence makes their summit views among the greatest on the planet.

The final Asian destination is, once again, utterly different. The dry, red, mystical landscapes of Wadi Rum in Jordan may feel almost alien. Desert nights under the brilliant stars, in a silence underscored by the wind whispering across the sand, are not to be forgotten. And just as the Everest region can hardly be understood without knowing its people, Rum's Bedouin are the best guides to being at home in the desert.

Mountain, steppe, rainforest, desert: it is, perhaps, just the beginning of a grasp on the enormity of Asia.

OVERLEAF *Yurts on the vast Mongolian steppe*

▽*Trekkers on the Burdah rock bridge*

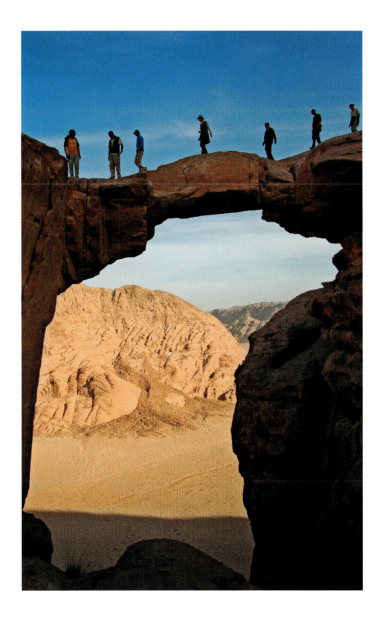

BORNEO
Climbing Mount Kinabalu

JON SPARKS

△ *Pitcher plant*

Mount Kinabalu (Gunung Kinabalu in Malay) is the highest mountain in South-east Asia, 4,095 m (13,436 ft) above sea level. Its upper reaches sprout pinnacles of naked granite but fortuitously the summit, known as Low's Peak, is without technical difficulty. The other peaks of the range are considerably more problematic. It's a compact and isolated range, with surrounding lands far below on every side, giving the summit views an even greater sense of elevation than you'd expect from a peak of this height.

The ascent is physically demanding but the slog up the lower slopes is enlivened by the incredible wealth and variety of the flora and fauna ; it is considered one of the world's premier biological sites.

The ascent starts from Park HQ at an altitude of 1,500 m (4,920 ft). Independent travellers will find that they're expected to hire a guide. This may be circumvented if you're determined, and prepared to sign a waiver form, but think carefully. Many conclude that using a local guide enhances the experience, bringing insight into the local culture, and gives something back to the local economy. The mountain is sacred to the local people and we climb with their permission. It's usually possible to share a guide with others.

Porters are also available if you have more gear than you can comfortably carry. All supplies for the overnight huts are carried on porters' backs and you're likely to be overtaken on the ascent by wiry figures burdened with propane bottles or hefty sacks of rice.

It's best to make an early start and pace yourself sensibly on the 2,000 m (6,560 ft) ascent to the overnight stop at Laban Rata. There are regular rest shelters, with water tanks. Take time to observe the changes as you pass through successive ecological zones from tropical rainforest to moss-hung cloudforest. There are belts of rhododendrons, more species of fern than the entire African continent, and distinctive insectivorous pitcher-plants.

You may be sweating as you arrive at Laban Rata, with the huge cliffs of Panar Laban looming behind the resthouse. It's prudent to dry off and change before settling down to refuel, or to enjoy the sunset views, as it's a lot colder than down below.

It's normal to make an 'Alpine start', often as early as 2 am. The aim is not to beat the crowds – everyone else does it too – but to beat the clouds which invariably gather around the summit later in the day. Feeling your way up by torchlight (a head-torch is best) there's only a vague, subliminal sense of the huge granite domes or of the lurking drops. Several sections involve hauling up fixed ropes, though they're not really difficult and hardened mountaineers may sneer at them. Glimpses of other tiny lights crawling up in the darkness, both above and below, convey some sense of the immensity of it all.

▽ *Walkers and*
St John's Peak

DESCRIPTION: 2-day arduous but non-technical ascent of a great isolated peak

LOCATION: Sabah, Malaysia, in northern regions of the island of Borneo

WHEN TO GO: year-round; temperatures vary little. The wet season is November – January and the dry season May – September, but heavy rain is possible at any time, particularly in the afternoons

START/FINISH: Kinabalu Park headquarters, served by regular buses from the capital, Kota Kinabalu

DURATION: normally 2 days, up and down.

MAX ALTITUDE: 4,095 m (13,436 ft)

ACCOMMODATION: resthouse at Laban Rata, providing beds, showers and simple food; more basic huts nearby. Hostel and restaurants adjacent to Park HQ at the foot of the mountain.

SPECIAL CONSIDERATIONS: be alert for signs of altitude sickness. Pack warm/waterproof clothing. A head-torch is very useful. Basic gear (torches, waterproofs) may be rented at Laban Rata. Trekking poles, and possibly sandals, recommended for the descent.

PERMITS/RESTRICTIONS: permits are required. Accommodation on the mountain must be booked before starting out

GUIDEBOOK: *Globetrotter Visitor's Guide Kinabalu Park* by Anthea Phillipps, pb New Holland (UK)

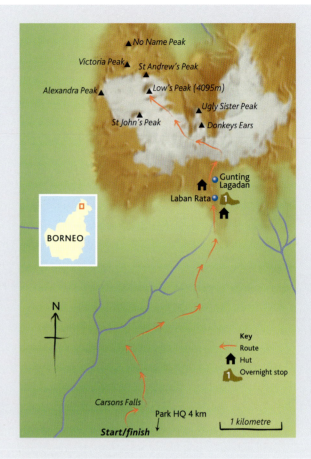

If you're going well you'll be on the bald summit slopes in the grey light before dawn, and on the summit in time to recover before the sun claws its way above the eastern horizon and the spectacle fully reveals itself. On clear days you can see skeins of islands strewn across the shimmering South China Sea. At this altitude, the distance to the horizon is over 200 km (125 miles) and you may feel you can see the curve of the Earth itself.

Going down is initially easier but, now that daylight's arrived, some find it rather more scary. There are spine-tingling glimpses of the awesome chasm known as Low's Gully, where a British Army expedition went missing in 1994. A quick breakfast back at Laban Rata and then most hurry on down back to the ordinary world. As this involves descending nearly 3000 m (9800 ft) in just a few hours, it can prove more painful than the ascent, especially if your boots don't fit perfectly. Some recommend swapping to trekking sandals for the descent to save the toes from a battering.

▷▷ *Mount Kinabalu*

THE HIMALAYA
The Everest Trek

KEV REYNOLDS

Thyangboche monastery stands upon a pine-clad ridge at 3,867 m (12,687 ft), an extravagant building which dwarfs the whitewashed monks' cells that surround it. During devotions, a deep rumble of voices drifts across the meadows, accompanied now and then by a blast of tuneless trumpets and the clash of cymbals. Unmoved, scavenging crows bounce across the grass among tethered yaks.

There may be more dramatic sites in the Himalaya, but this is one of the most sublime, for Thyangboche commands an eye-watering sample of natural wonders with which the Khumbu region of Nepal is so generously endowed. Ama Dablam bestows a benediction nearby, Thamserku and Kantega rise to the south, while in the north an immense wall stretches between Nuptse and Lhotse, overlooked by the summit cone of Everest.

▽ *On the first stage from Lukla, a suspension bridge over the Dudh Kosi leads to the lodges of Phakding*

It's impossible to gaze on such a scene and remain unmoved.

The most popular trek to the world's highest mountain overnights in one of the Thyangboche lodges, about four days after landing at the Lukla airstrip. Though it's possible to make the journey to Everest and back in two weeks, to experience this Himalayan wonderland properly, allow a minimum of three weeks.

It takes 1.5 days to walk from Lukla to the Sherpa 'capital' of Namche Bazaar, crossing and recrossing the Dudh Kosi river several times. Waterfalls spray from narrow clefts flanked by massive rock walls; at Ghat signs of the Buddhist faith line the trail – mani stones, a gompa, man-sized prayer wheels, and a flotilla of prayer flags catching the wind. At Mondzo you enter the Sagarmatha National Park, and later cross a suspension bridge high above the river to begin the long steep climb to Namche, a real test of fitness and acclimatization for the first-time Himalayan trekker.

Saturday is Namche's big day, for the weekly market is in full swing with Sherpas, porters and Tibetan traders striking bargains and exchanging wares. Built against a steep curving hillside at the confluence of the Dudh Kosi and Bhote Kosi at 3,445 m (11,306 ft),

△ *Ama Dablam appears as a double-headed peak when seen from the moraine crest above Dingboche*

107

the township is stocked with trekkers' lodges, restaurants, a post office, bank, money exchange facilities and even a dental clinic. The National Park headquarters is located on a spur close by, and the two nights spent acclimatizing here will fly past.

On leaving Namche a short morning's walk leads to Sanasa, a string of teahouses at a trail junction. One route breaks left, bound for the Gokyo valley, while the Everest trail descends to the river at Phunki Tenga. After crossing a flag-bedecked bridge you begin the 600 m (2,000 ft) climb to Thyangboche where both the views and the atmosphere make it an unforgettable resting place.

▽ *This small icy lake at Gorak Shep lies at the foot of Kalar Pattar, with the Khumbu valley's headwall serving as a backdrop*

Setting out next day the trail inevitably winds downhill, this time to cross another suspension bridge on the way to Pangboche, a Sherpa village built on two levels. In the upper village, the oldest of the Khumbu gompas is worth a visit before continuing upvalley and, passing below Ama Dablam, you reach the confluence of the Imja Khola and Khumbu Khola. Although the route to Everest base camp swings left, it's preferable to take the right branch to spend a night or two in Dingboche, a less windy option than Pheriche which lies on the other side of an intervening moraine.

Behind Dingboche a high trail cuts along the flank of Pokalde and joins the lower trail at Duglha, from where you ascend the Khumbu glacier's terminal moraine and arrive at the busy lodge village of Lobuche at 4,930 m (16,175 ft). Though there are lodges at Gorak Shep, about 1.5-2 hours' trekking distance away, they're spartan and with poor sanitation, so most trekkers make a long day's hike from Lobuche to the vantage point of Kala Pattar and return, carrying only their essentials.

Everest Base Camp? To the uninitiated this may seem like the ultimate destination, but since Everest itself cannot be seen, by far the better option is to branch left at Gorak Shep and make the ascent of Kalar Pattar, 5,623 m (18,448 ft) to enjoy one of the world's truly great views. Across the valley to the east soars the black pyramid of Everest, with the even more impressive ice-pleated face of Nuptse close by. Pumori rises directly above you, the Khumbu glacier below, and a 360° panorama of natural wonders includes Lingtren, Ama Dablam, Thamserku and Kangtega.

Your lungs may be rasping, your breath laboured, but with such beauty all around, it's worth every moment.

DESCRIPTION: high altitude trek among sky-scratching peaks to Kalar Pattar for a panorama of awesome grandeur dominated by the highest mountain on earth

WHEN TO GO: October to December, or March to April

START/FINISH: Lukla, reached by plane from Kathmandu

FINISH: Lukla – this is a there-and-back trek, although variations are possible

DURATION: a minimum of 2 weeks, but preferably 3 to explore side valleys

MAX ALTITUDE: 5623 m (18,448 ft) on Kalar Pattar

ACCOMMODATION: simple trekkers' lodges throughout

SPECIAL CONSIDERATIONS: it's essential to allow time to acclimatize properly. Note that sub-zero night temperatures are the norm beyond Thyangboche. Be suitably clothed and with good down sleeping bags

PERMITS/RESTRICTIONS: entry permits (obtained at Mondzo) are needed for the Sagarmatha National Park

GUIDEBOOK: *Everest: A Trekker's Guide* by Kev Reynolds, pb Cicerone Press

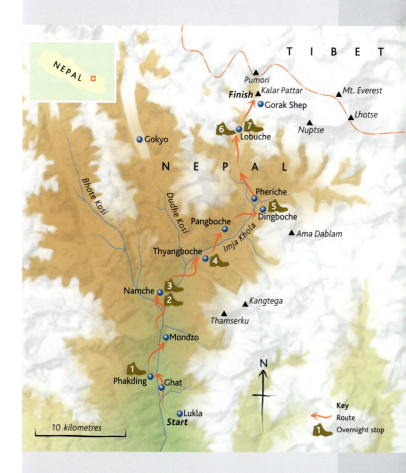

UVS AIMAG
Kharkhiraa – Yamaatiin Trek

JON SPARKS

For space, Mongolia is beyond compare. With a population of little more than two million, this vast land-locked country is the most thinly-peopled on Earth. Mongolia's landscapes of vast green plains and enormous skies are hauntingly like the image of the American prairies of old. Here there are no buffalo, only sheep, goats and camels, but here there are also people who still live the life of nomads, a life centred on the horse.

In some regions the plains seem to stretch off to infinity but elsewhere, especially in the west, they rise to rounded, grass-draped hills and then to snowy peaks. Apart from the mountains ranged along the horizon, this feels like – and very largely is – a land without boundaries, a quality that that a visitor from more crowded lands may find initially strange but which is, ultimately, utterly liberating.

These western reaches offer exhilarating, but not overly difficult, trekking to and through the mountains. The waving grasses and the trails of the nomads' herds give generally easy walking, leaving you free to luxuriate in the intoxicating space and the clarity of the air.

Given the distance and other logistical hurdles, it's inevitable that most visitors will opt for an organised trek and these are now offered by a good range of companies. In most cases the heavy loads are carried by pack animals, either horses or camels, which is far more fitting than relying on vehicles.

The Mongolian nomad's traditional home is the yurt – more correctly called the ger – which is rather more substantial than your average tent. Gers don't lend themselves to being moved daily, so it's more likely that you'll be sleeping in more conventional tents but may have a ger as mess tent, or get the chance to visit one.

Itineraries vary, but the following route is fairly typical and takes in most of the highlights of the region. The size, and the emptiness, begin to sink in on the journey from Ulanbataar to the regional capital of Ulaangom – a three-hour flight, and a multi-day epic by any other means of transport. There'll probably be a visit to the National Parks Centre,

▽ *Part of a Mongolian camel train*

△ *Herding yaks*

as the trek ventures into the Turgen Strictly Protected Area, home to one of the world's largest populations of snow leopard. It's highly unlikely that you'll actually see this most beautiful and elusive of big cats, but it's always worth keeping your eyes open.

There's usually a short drive from here to the start of the trek in the Kharkhiraa Valley. Morning chill and the grumbling of camels drive home the reality of the fabled land. For the first couple of days, the walking is easy, gradually ascending the broad valley past scattered encampments and ancient grave-sites. There are uplifting views of Mount Turgen, but it's not until the end of this phase that Mount Kharkiraa, with its dramatic ice-cliffs, shoulders into view. The moraines and rock ridges above the green valley are good places to spot argali (wild sheep), but it's that slender chance of sighting a snow leopard that gives a real tingle of anticipation.

There's a rough but fairly short climb to the 2,974 m (9,758 ft) Kharkiraa Pass, gateway to a rolling alpine upland under Kharkiraa and Turgen; views also extend to the highest peaks of the Altai range, several of which top 4,000 m (13,120 ft), looking sharp and close in the clear air. On a calm day, the precisely-named Blue Lake is a perfect mirror. There's a

DESCRIPTION: sustained trekking on mostly easy terrain of vast grassy plains and Alpine plateaus overlooked by glaciated peaks

LOCATION: Uvs Aimaq (Aimaq = province) in western Mongolia

WHEN TO GO: Mongolia has a short summer, extending little beyond July and August

START/FINISH: treks normally start from the regional capital Ulaangom

DURATION: approx 9 days trekking

MAX ALTITUDE: 3,147 m (10,325 ft)

ACCOMMODATION: camping; all camp gear normally carried by camels or horses

SPECIAL CONSIDERATIONS: warm sleeping bag and clothing needed as nights can be very cold

PERMITS/RESTRICTIONS: National Park permits needed

GUIDEBOOK: *Mongolia* by Michael Kohn, pb Lonely Planet

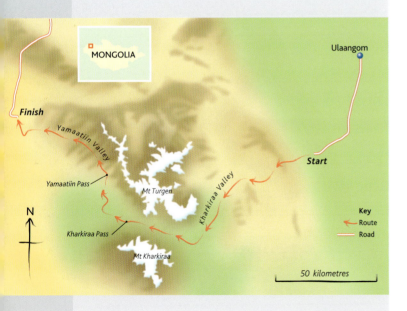

high camp before the crossing of the 3,147 m (10,325 ft) Yamaatiin Pass and descent into the remote, pristine Yamaatiin valley. It's common – and sensible – to include a 'rest' day here, though it's often spent climbing back up onto the bounding ridges. Spectacular views are guaranteed, while sightings of ibex and argali may reward a slow, patient, approach.

◁◁ *Snow leopard*

The trek continues for another day or two down the Yamaatiin valley; the absence of humans, or their animals, leaves the grasses lush and rich in flowers. Lower down the valley, there are pine forests reminiscent of the Pyrenees or the High Sierra.

The trek ends, far too soon, at a roadhead. Transfer to a jeep comes as a rude shock after the days of pure air, unsullied by the sound or stink of engines. It's common to spend a final night on the shores of stunning Lake Uureg, close to the Russian border, before the return to Ulaangom.

▽ *The Kharkhiraa Valley*

Wadi Rum

JON SPARKS

Some places call to the walker simply because they're gorgeous. Others have the allure of legend. The very best, of course, do both.

Such a place is Wadi Rum, famed for its associations with Lawrence of Arabia (T E Lawrence). In fact Lawrence made only brief visits. His *Seven Pillars of Wisdom* is indigestible to modern readers, and the myth is fuelled mostly by David Lean's magnificent but sometimes misleading 1962 movie. Beyond doubt, however, Lawrence was bewitched by Wadi Rum, calling it 'this irresistible place: this processional way greater than imagination.'

▽ *Camels in the desert under the northern walls of Jebel um Ishrin*

Wadi Rum is the name of a valley – Lawrence's 'processional way' – but applies also to a 720 square kilometres (280 sq miles) Protected Area. Sandstone mountains leap without prelude from the brick-red sand. These great walls make Wadi Rum an international rock-climbing hotspot, but many summits are beyond the reach of walkers.

Wadi Rum today is on the tourist trail, with a smart new visitor centre and innumerable options for tours by camel or today's 'Ship of the Desert', a battered Toyota Landcruiser. But rattling around in a stuffy cab is no way to experience Wadi Rum: travelling on foot is a far richer experience. Like Lawrence, you may find, 'Our little caravan grew self-conscious, and fell dead quiet, afraid and ashamed to flaunt its smallness in the presence of the stupendous hills.'

Wadi Rum is a maze of mountains, broad wadis and slot-like canyons or siqs. The choice of routes is vast. Start, perhaps, from the green oasis of Disseh, easily across gritty desert, peaks slowly solidifying out of the haze. Walls grow ever more improbable until a seeming dead-end reveals the cool cleft of Siq Burrah. Effigies of Lawrence and his comrade Faisal are carved into a rock at the Umm Twaggy campsite.

△ *Bedouin guide, Wadi Rum*

Next morning the way winds through the siq for several hours before emerging into desert dazzle. From looming verticals to wide horizontals; the transition is almost shocking. Cross low sandstone slabs and open sand to a secluded campsite. A short morning's hike gains the foot of Jebel Burdah. An intricate but rarely difficult route scrambles up Burdah's convoluted flanks to its famous rock bridge. The final pitch below the bridge is awkward and exposed, but crossing the arch itself requires only a fair head for heights. On the long descent the rocks glow in the sinking sun.

After Burdah comes more easy desert walking. Another rock bridge at Um Frouth is more accessible, but equally preposterous. Continue under the blank purple walls of Jebel Khazali, and round its northern end. Here lurks Siq Khazali, where startling pools reflect a sliver of sky. In deep recesses, protected by overhangs, are inscriptions from the Nabatean civilization, pre-dating the Romans.

Across the desert to another camp, tucked under tiered rock ledges ideal for sunset-gazing. Bedouin songs around the crackling fire; the velvet sky thronged with stars; the softness of sand under the mattress; goat-hair tent walls flapping softly in the breeze.

OVERLEAF *Trekkers on a vast sand dune, Wadi Rum*

▷ *A traditional Bedouin tent, woven from goat hair, tucked under a rock wall*

facts and figures

DESCRIPTION: easy trekking through narrow canyons and across open desert, under implausible sandstone peaks, with optional spectacular scrambling

LOCATION: Wadi Rum Protected Area in southern Jordan

WHEN TO GO: open all year, but summer days can be very hot and winter nights below freezing. Spring and autumn are most comfortable but also busiest

START/FINISH: Rum Visitor Centre, Rum village or Disseh village. Sporadic bus service or taxi from the resort of Aqaba, about 45 km (28 miles) away

DURATION: described trek is 5 days/4 nights; many other options available

MAX ALTITUDE: on described trek, approx. 1,350 m (4,430 ft) at Burdah rock bridge

ACCOMMODATION: on trek, accommodation is often in traditional Bedouin tents; beds are occasionally provided but sleeping on the sand, with a foam pad, is more comfortable. Treks are usually vehicle-supported. Rum village has a rest-house and backpacker hostel. There is talk of building a hotel by the Visitor Centre

SPECIAL CONSIDERATIONS: wear modest clothing in villages and around Bedouin camps. Good sun protection advisable. It is advisable to book guides etc. in advance

PERMITS/RESTRICTIONS: all visitors must pay entry fee at the Visitor Centre.

GUIDEBOOK: *Treks & Climbs in Wadi Rum Jordan* by Tony Howard, pb Cicerone Press

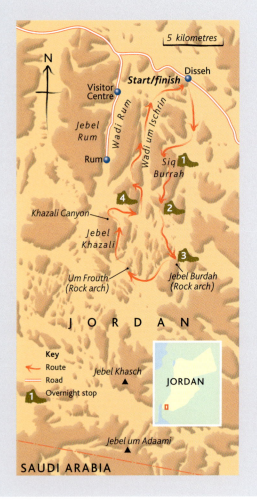

It's a crowded last day, past the hidden, cave-like 'Lawrence's House', then a diversion to climb a monstrous red dune – and bound down again in a fifth of the time. Then there's the chance to ride a camel, swaying along under the walls of Wadi um Ishrin, before returning to Disseh.

Wadi Rum may haunt you, as it did Lawrence, and there's much to return for; Rum itself, planted between 500 m (1,600 ft) cliffs, is a good base for more desert walks. Or you can range further south, where the sand turns white and far fewer visitors reach, to scale the tangled domes of Jebel Khasch or the ragged ridges of Jebel Um Adaami, Jordan's highest peak at 1,830 m (6,004 ft). From the summit, endless ridges – each a little fainter than the last – recede far into Saudi Arabia. Or perhaps into imagination.

▽ *View from high on Jebel Burdah towards Jebel um Ischrin*

AUSTRALIA AND NEW ZEALAND

"There is such a lot to find in it, but such a lot of it to find it in."

BILL BRYSON

△ *Cradle Mountain range, Tasmania*

Australia is an anomaly. Is it the world's smallest continent, or its largest island? And if it is a continent, where do islands like New Zealand fit in? Terms like Australasia and Oceania are not rooted in physical reality, just convenient ways of lumping together various lands that (from the other side of the earth) appear fairly close together.

In fact Australia and New Zealand, separated by more than a thousand miles of deep ocean, are different in almost every way, except their colonial and post-colonial history. Australia is geologically old and stable: if it is a continent, it is the only one without active volcanoes. New Zealand is young and active, part of the 'Ring of Fire' encircling the Pacific. There are similar disparities in flora and fauna; in each case, eighty percent of native species are found nowhere else. Their original people are equally different. New Zealand's Maori came to the islands from Polynesia, probably less than a millennium ago. No-one knows for sure where Australia's Aboriginal people came from, but they have been there at least forty thousand years and possibly substantially longer.

What's more, Australia's Aborigines are arguably the greatest walkers the world has ever known. Not only did they colonise this vast island/continent without the help of animals to ride or carry loads, but walking was also central to their culture, to their very existence. Their entire culture, from mythology to the most mundane practical knowledge, was relayed through stories and songs which were told and retold as the people walked across the land. Particular stories belonged in particular places.

Much of Australia's interior – the 'Outback' – appears desolate and virtually featureless to outsiders, though rich in meaning to its indigenous people. Fortunately, 'featureless' is not a word that applies to the rugged quartzite spines of the Macdonnell Ranges, in Australia's Red Centre, where the Larapinta Trail winds its course.

The Blue Mountains of New South Wales are different in almost every way; a barrier to rainfall sweeping in from the Tasman Sea, and for some decades a barrier to European expansion across the land. Lush vegetation, or 'bush', abounds, except where the crags are too steep.

Tasmania may look like a mere afterthought off Australia's southernmost shore, but it is as large as Ireland. 'Tas' boasts that it is the only part of Australia to have four distinct seasons, and also claims the world's cleanest air. In its southwestern corner, jagged peaks dominate one of the most important temperate wilderness areas in the southern hemisphere.

New Zealand may also look small on the world map, but has incredible physical diversity, from sub-tropical lushness in the north to glaciated peaks in South Island. Picking one walk to represent New Zealand is well-nigh impossible, but the simmering volcanic plateau at the centre of North Island is not to be missed.

Australia and New Zealand may be chalk and cheese, but still have much in common: vast spaces, powerful landscapes, and the awesome night skies of the southern hemisphere.

OVERLEAF *Walkers at the summit of Red Crater, on New Zealand's Tongariro Crossing*

▽ *Ormiston Gorge, The Larapinta Trail, Northern Territory*

TASMANIA
The Overland Track, Cradle Mountain

CAMERON M. BURNS

▷▷ *Lake Dove, Cradle Mountain–Lake St. Clair National Park*

▽ *Alpine forest at Waterfall Valley, Cradle Mountain–Lake St. Clair National Park*

Geologists cite Tasmania as a prime place to examine dolerite, a coarse-grained basaltic rock that often takes unusual forms. My geologist father spent much of his youth wandering the Tasmanian bush, never tiring of its many dolerite cliffs, crags, and intrusions. But even he'd agree that this sparkling dark rock attains its grandest forms in the mountains. Nowhere on earth does dolerite rise in such proud majesty as in Cradle Mountain – Lake St. Clair National Park. And the best way to see the park is, of course, by walking the Overland Track. This is truly one of the world's greatest walks.

Why?

One word: its wild-ness.

The national park lies within UNESCO's Tasmanian Wilderness World Heritage Area, which covers roughly one-fifth of the island. The place has hardly seen the hand of man. Just a generation ago, some maps still labelled the entire southwest of Tasmania as 'unexplored.' Somehow, Tasmanians have protected much of the region from the logging companies that have razed vast forests elsewhere on the island.

The track starts at Ronny Creek in Cradle Valley, home to gregarious wallabies. It passes Crater Falls and Crater Lake, then skirts picturesque Lake Dove and climbs to Marion's Lookout (the biggest ascent of the walk) on the Cradle Plateau. This section is called the 'Goat Track' for the steep scramble around the eastern side of Crater Lake; the alternative 'Horse Track' skirts to the west.

DESCRIPTION: seven days' walking across rugged mountain terrain, staying in small mountain huts

LOCATION: Tasmania, Australia, in the high centre west of the island

WHEN TO GO: walkable year round, but can experience very severe weather in winter. December – March is the favoured period and February usually the best month

START: Ronny Creek, served by buses from Cradle Mountain visitors' centre

FINISH: Cynthia Bay, on Lake St. Clair

DURATION: 65 km (40 miles), typically 6 or 7 days. Add another very short day if walking between Cradle Mountain visitors' centre and Dove Lake, and another day if walking the length of Lake St. Clair instead of taking the ferry

MAX ALTITUDE: 1,250 m (4,101 ft)

ACCOMMODATION: first-come, first-served rustic mountain huts (no amenities) although all walkers are advised to bring tents

SPECIAL CONSIDERATIONS: in winter, full mountaineering clothing and a tent are strongly recommended. Campfires aren't allowed and the huts' stoves are inadequate; bring a camp stove

PERMITS/RESTRICTIONS: in high season (November 1 – April 30), booking and Park entry fees are required, plus $100 fee for those doing the full Overland Track, and hikers must travel north to south. At other times the track is free and open to hikers in both directions. See www.overlandtrack.com.au. No more than 60 walkers are allowed to depart each day from Cradle Mountain

GUIDEBOOK: *Walking in Australia* by Andrew Bain, et al., pb Lonely Planet

Start ● Ronnie Creek
Marions Lookout
Crater Lake
Dove Lake
🏠 Kitchen Hut

TASMANIA

Waterfall Valley huts
🏠 **1**

Barn Bluff ▲

🏠 **2** Windemere Hut

Mount Oakleigh ▲

Pine Forest Moor
🏠 Pelion huts
3

Mount Ossa ▲

4
Kia Oro huts 🏠
Du Cane hut 🏠

Windy
Ridge Hut 🏠 **5**

Key
← Route
🏠 Hut
1 Overnight stop

Narcissus Bay ● *Finish*

Lake St Clair

|__10 kilometres__|

The majestic dolerite stump of Barn Bluff appears and within an hour so does Kitchen Hut, a rough emergency shelter. The trail continues past the Cradle Mountain summit track and Fury Gorge and descends to the Waterfall Valley huts.

A side trip to Barn Bluff fills an easy and enjoyable morning before heading off for the Windemere Hut. Below Barn Bluff, the trail passes spoil from the pelionite oil shale mines (decades ago, lumps of pelionite lay about; easily lit, they were a favorite campfire fuel). Crossing sedgeland moors with several picturesque glacial tarns, the spires of Mount Oakleigh loom to the southeast.

The third day is widely considered the hardest, with extremely rough sections over bogs and rocky terrain. It begins by climbing to Pine Forest Moor, where bogs are traversed on boardwalks, before entering a low-wooded area, crosses Pelion Creek (which pours off the 1,560 m/5,118 ft Mount Pelion West), and descends to Frog Flats. Crossing the River Forth, the way leads east to Pelion Plains and the Pelion huts. At the old Douglas Creek copper mines nearby, sparkling chalcopyrite ore can be found.

Now the walk follows Douglas Creek and climbs to Pelion Gap, 1,125 m (3,691 ft), then southeast past the brooding walls of Mount Ossa, 1,617 m (5,305 ft), a magnificent hunk of dolerite and Tasmania's tallest peak. (A side trail leads from Pelion Gap to the summit.) The Pinestone Valley descends to Kia Oro Creek and the Kia Oro huts.

Tracking southeast through eucalyptus scrub, the century-old Du Cane hut – former home of a trapper – is soon reached. Here the Mersey River tumbles over a series of falls, all just east of the track. The trail climbs to Du Cane Gap, then descends to Windy Ridge Hut.

From here descend gradually to a flat valley bottom and on to Narcissus Bay on Lake St Clair. A ferry takes walkers to the Cynthia Bay visitors' centre, where a shuttle can be caught back to the start.

Along this hike, you'll see rocks from every geological period, the oldest formed about 1,100 million years ago during the Precambrian. It's a great trip into the bush, and natural history. But it's the dolerite that'll grab your attention the most.

△ Crater Falls, Cradle Mountain–Lake St. Clair National Park

◁◁ The iconic peak of Barn Bluff

THE BLUE MOUNTAINS
The Six-Foot Track

CAMERON M. BURNS

Narratives of the early European exploration of Australia are filled with harsh battles against the elements, shy and fearful natives, and a dizzying sense of the unknown. Even the early attempts to get as far as Paramatta, a modern suburb of western Sydney, saw explorers struggling for weeks to penetrate the thick unyielding bush. This was difficult enough, but for several decades the real question was 'what's over those mountains?' The mountains, of course, were the Blue Mountains, comprising more than a million hectares (3,900 sq miles) of sandstone plateaus, gorges, and canyons, all covered by a lush temperate eucalyptus forest.

▽ *Megalong Valley*

Finding a way across the mountains became something of a national obsession as soldiers, pastoralists, scientists, and the generally curious were defeated by the complex geography. One of the greatest exploratory feats in the young colony's history came when, in 1813, explorers Gregory Blaxland, Henry Lawson and William Wentworth managed, in seventeen days, to hack, push, and fight their way through the mountains to the fertile Western Tableland of New South Wales. Today, the three are national heroes, with various natural features, settlements, and buildings named for them.

It's possible to get a notion of what they experienced on the Six-Foot Track (named for the then required width of a bridle path), a three-day walk through some of the rugged country they first explored. The Track follows an 1884 horse track from Katoomba to Jenolan, one of Australia's first and still biggest natural tourist attractions. It starts at the famed Explorer's Tree (which has the initials of Blaxland, Lawson and Wentworth carved upon it) about 2 km (1.25 miles) west of Katoomba along the Great Western Highway.

From the tree, there's a short walk through the bush to the descent into Nellie's Glen. The descent down steep wooden steps can take up to an hour, and needs care, especially if wet. Passing Bonnie Doon Falls, the track continues into the Megalong Valley, with the sheer yellow/orange walls of the Narrow Neck Plateau rising to the southeast. It was such seemingly endless walls – which riddle the Blue Mountains – that halted early explorers.

The valley is noticeably drier than the plateau and scribbly gums (named for the strange lines on their bark) dominate. Soon, the track reaches Megalong Village, home to coal and shale miners in the early twentieth century; the mines themselves were under the Narrow Neck Plateau.

The track now follows Megalong Creek through rolling farmland. Reaching the Cox's River Valley, the vegetation becomes more typical woodland again. The day ends with a crossing of the river via the Bowtells Swing Bridge – a narrow 90 m (300 ft) cable suspension bridge – then a short stroll to the Cox's River campsite.

OVERLEAF *View of Three Sisters, near Katoomba*

▽ *Nellie's Glen*

△ *View of the Blue Mountains with its famous eucalyptus forest*

▷▷ *Jenolan Caves*

Day two starts with a 300 m (1,000 ft) climb up to a relatively flat area where an old homestead, Kyangatha, is located, followed by another 200 m (660 ft) climb up to and over the Mini Mini Saddle. Here you re-enter the woodlands and descend to Alum Creek. Then the trail climbs again to the Black Range, which is followed for 11 km (6.8 miles). This is the highest section of the track and certain species of snow gums can be seen. The last camp, the Black Range campsite, has an open shelter, a composting toilet, and a water tank.

The last day starts through the bush to Jenolan Road; the Track parallels the road past Binda Flat and continues on another 4 km (2.5 miles) to the popular Jenolan Caves. As this last day is quite short, there is time to explore. To return to Katoomba requires either retracing the route or catching one of several walkers' shuttles. Not surprisingly, the Six-Foot Track is one of the more popular treks in Australia, as it takes the walker through several distinct ecosystems with their own mammals, birds, and reptiles — indeed, more than 50 bird species have been identified along the track. And it's a true hike, climbing a total of 1,530 m (5,020 ft) and dropping a total 1,789 m (5,870 ft). Not bad on a flat continent!

DESCRIPTION: Three days' supported trekking or backpacking through rugged Australian bush terrain, following a historic track

LOCATION: New South Wales, Australia, about 100 km west of Sydney

WHEN TO GO: Year-round, although many prefer the Australian winter as the route is more likely to have available water

START: Katoomba, New South Wales

FINISH: Jenolan, home to one of Australia's finest limestone caverns

DURATION: Typically 3 days (45 km/28 miles)

MAX ALTITUDE: 1,215 m (3,980 ft) at the Jenolan Road crossing

ACCOMMODATION: Two nights bush camping at established campgrounds; greater choice at the start and end-points

SPECIAL CONSIDERATIONS: The walk can be very dry; be prepared to carry plenty of water

PERMITS/RESTRICTIONS: Individuals and small family groups do not need bookings. Larger groups must register in advance with the Six-Foot Track Heritage Trust. Campfires are banned

GUIDEBOOK: *Walking in Australia* (5th edition) by Andrew Bain *et. al.*, pb Lonely Planet

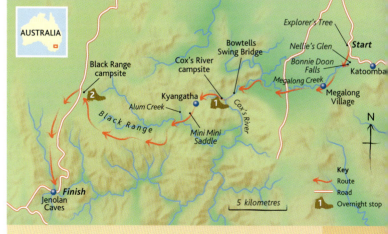

AUSTRALIA

Black Range campsite

Cox's River campsite

Bowtells Swing Bridge

Explorer's Tree

Nellie's Glen **Start**

Bonnie Doon Falls

Megalong Creek

Katoomba

Kyangatha

Alum Creek

Black Range

Mini Mini Saddle

Cox's River

Megalong Village

N

Finish

Jenolan Caves

5 kilometres

Key

Route

Road

Overnight stop

DESCRIPTION: long trek across hot, red, ancient ridges and through dry river valleys

LOCATION: The Macdonnell ranges, west of Alice Springs, Northern Territory, Australia

WHEN TO GO: Summer is excessively hot; the recommended season is April – October

START: Alice Springs Telegraph Station

FINISH: Redbank Gorge, below Mt Sonder

DURATION: The full trail is 223 km (139 miles) and takes from 15 – 20 days; described section is 5 days / 4 nights

MAX ALTITUDE: 1,331 m (4,367 ft) on Mt Sonder

ACCOMMODATION: sections can be done as day-walks from a base at Alice Springs or Glen Helen Resort. As a continuous trek, camping is the only option, sleeping in tents or swags. Fully supported treks are available, as are food-drops for backpackers

SPECIAL CONSIDERATIONS/EQUIPMENT NEEDED: Good sun protection is vital. Backpackers need to carry large volumes of water on some stages. Winter nights can be well below freezing

PERMITS/RESTRICTIONS: camping is limited to designated sites. Park/camping fees apply at some of these

GUIDEBOOK: *Walking in Australia* by Andrew Bain *et. al.*, pb Lonely Planet

deep, permanent pools. High ledges are home to a colony of wallabies.

From Ormiston Gorge, the way winds south-west through low, chaotic hills, then down into the wide channel of Ormiston Creek. Normally dry, its sandy bed makes a broad walkers' highway. Deep-buried water sustains the tall River Red Gum trees.

Ormiston Creek feeds into the broader, but equally dry, Finke River. Here, shallow pools, permanent except in the worst of droughts, support a vibrant wildlife. Burrowing frogs breed when the rains come and survive between times in a kind of stasis deep underground. From here you can walk 4.5 km (2.8 miles) to Glen Helen Resort, where you can sleep in a bed. But it's

hard to beat lying cosy on the sand in a swag, listening to the distant howling of dingoes, or peering out at the Milky Way – more dazzling than ever in the northern hemisphere.

The next stage runs mostly flat, bar a mid-way climb onto another hilltop lookout. The sweeping curves of the Davenport River are dry, but subsurface aquifers make this area unusually lush with waving golden grasses. The sight of two Red Kangaroos, mother and youngster, skimming across the flats in early light, is seared into memory for ever.

And so to Rwetyepme itself. The long west ridge gathers itself as it rises. At half-height it's almost breached by an abrupt slash of a gully that draws the gaze down and out over a great level expanse of bush; cattle country, though the home station is far away beyond the next ridge. The scrubby ridge turns to naked rock at the south summit, crags falling away on the east side, revealing a view back over the ridges of the preceding days.

The connection to the main summit is difficult and exposed and in any case it's off-limits. The entire mountain is sacred to the Arrernte; access is by consent and it is vital that visitors show respect and don't stray from the agreed route. This land is theirs, if anyone's.

▽ *Looking west from Count's Point, with Mount Sonder on the horizon*

NORTH ISLAND
Ascent of Mt Ruapehu and the Tongariro Crossing

JON SPARKS

Three great volcanic peaks, Tongariro, Ngauruhoe and Ruapehu, rear from the Central Plateau of New Zealand's North Island. So sacred were they to the region's Maori people that those passing by were required to shield their eyes. To protect the area from crass development in the 19th century, Paramount Chief Te Heuheu Tukino IV chose to make a gift of the land to all the nation's people, personified by Queen Victoria. Thus, Tongariro became the first National Park in the southern hemisphere and the fourth in the world.

All the peaks still simmer with activity; in places the ground trembles underfoot like a pan about to boil. Walking possibilities are legion, and the multi-day Round the Mountains Track is one of the Department of Conservation's 'Great Walks'. It's also possible to take in the highlights in a couple of one-day walks.

Ruapehu, at 2,797 m (9,177 ft), is the highest peak on North Island, but access is easy via the Whakapapa ski-field; you can take a bus to 1,630 m (5,348 ft) and then chairlifts half-way to the summit. When the snow disappears, much of the terrain is not the bulldozed pistes of the typical European resort, but bare black rock. Easy scrambling, past scraps of old snow and ice, leads over Knoll Ridge and Restful Ridge to the rim of the Summit Plateau.

This is a treacherous-looking wasteland of mud, snow and ice; it's best to keep to the rim, with the sad remnant of the Whakapapa Glacier below on the other side, rising to Dome Ridge. Dome Summit, at 2,660 m (8,727 ft), is the usual stopping-point for walkers; the continuation to Tahurangi, the true summit, is for mountaineers only.

Still, Dome Summit is a marvellous place, overlooking the cauldron of Crater Lake, which vanished in the eruption of 1995 but has since refilled. The high ridges also offer staggering views. 1,800 m (6,000 ft) below, green plains roll into the distance. If you're lucky, you can see North Island's other great volcano, Taranaki, 130 km (80 miles) away.

The ascent of Ruapehu is memorable, but the Tongariro Crossing is utterly unforgettable. Inevitably it's popular, and the logistics of transport mean that most people start the walk at around the same time, but the line soon stretches and any sense of crowding is dispelled by the wide, brooding landscape.

A gentle opening follows the Mangatepopo Stream, skirting black, contorted lava. After a steep, rocky climb to Mangatepopo Saddle, there's a choice. Ngauruhoe or not? Its scored slopes rear up 600 m (2,000 ft) in blatant challenge, and at 2,291m (7,517 ft) it's the highest point of the Tongariro massif.

It's a challenge often declined, but the rewards are immense. An hour or more of treadmill ascent yields to abrupt arrival at the rim of the crater; a great pit, where wispy

▽ *Mount Ruapehu*

▷*Tongariro's Red Crater*

facts and figures

DESCRIPTION: day walks in magnificent volcanic surroundings

LOCATION: Tongariro National Park, North Island, New Zealand

WHEN TO GO: the summer season is December – March. The routes are possible all year but may require winter equipment

START/FINISH: The Ruapehu ascent starts and finishes at Whakapapa. The Tongariro Crossing starts at Mangatepopo and finishes at Okahukura. Local accommodation providers offer shuttle service for these points

DURATION: ½ day for Ruapehu; full day for Tongariro

MAX ALTITUDE: 2,660m (8,727 ft)

ACCOMMODATION: wide choice in the area. Mountain huts available for longer walks

SPECIAL CONSIDERATIONS/EQUIPMENT NEEDED: be prepared for changeable weather and/or volcanic fumes. Volcanic activity can change or occasionally close the tracks: check local information before setting out

PERMITS/RESTRICTIONS: none

GUIDEBOOK: *Tramping in New Zealand* by Jim Dufresne, pb Lonely Planet

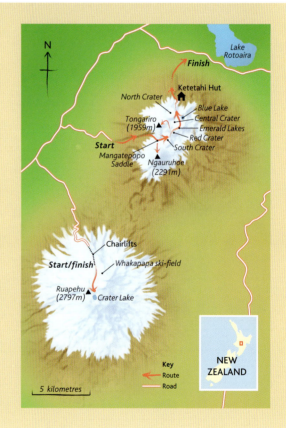

N

Lake Rotoaira

Finish

Ketetahi Hut

North Crater

Blue Lake
Central Crater
Tongariro (1959m)▲
Emerald Lakes
Red Crater

Start
Mangatepopo Saddle
South Crater
Ngauruhoe (2291m)

Chairlifts
Start/finish
Whakapapa ski-field

Ruapehu (2797m)▲ ●Crater Lake

Key
→ Route
— Road

NEW ZEALAND

5 kilometres

yellow fumes rise among rocks that echo all the colours of fire. Unlike at Ruapehu, here there are true 360-degree views.

△ Looking down to Emerald Lakes from Red Crater

The descent takes mere minutes, if you know how to scree-run, and then there's the Martian emptiness of South Crater. Climb onto the rim of Central Crater. If there's an hour to spare, take in the 1,967 m (6,454 ft) summit of Tongariro. Otherwise, press on to Red Crater, the most active area on the massif. The ground seethes underfoot; steam leaks from innumerable vents; the sulphurous stink can be overpowering. Nothing feels entirely solid.

A steep, loose descent follows, to Emerald Lakes. You might say they are really just large pools; you might say they are turquoise, rather than the pure green the name implies; but who cares? Drink in the scene, the stark contrast with the crater's chaos of reds, whites and blacks: just don't drink the water itself.

Central Crater is black desolation, followed by a short climb and descent to Blue Lake. One last brief climb and then there's a 9,00m (3,000 ft) descent to finish. Views stretch over Lake Taupo, in its vast caldera. Its explosive birth – equivalent to a hundred Krakatoas – is reliably dated to 186 AD, coinciding with records of darkened daytime skies and bloody sunsets from both China and Rome.

Continue the descent past Ketetahi Hut and down into bush. This return to the living world brings welcome shade and a chance to reflect, to begin to assimilate the other-worldly experience of the Tongariro crossing.

NORTH AMERICA

"I have seen how the foundations of the world are laid, and I have not the least doubt that it will stand a good while."

HENRY DAVID THOREAU

△ *Sun shining over Grand Canyon, Arizona*

Thanks largely to Hollywood, and above all the Western, North America's landscapes are familiar to more of the world's population than any other continent. Magnificently iconic the landscapes of the 'Wild West' may be, but there's far more to North America: great mountains, surf-battered coasts, and above all vast tracts of forest. The Western may paint a picture of travel on horseback, but across the whole continent exploration on foot and by canoe are historically far more significant. Today it is as true here as anywhere else that walking gives an unmatched sense of the grandeur of great landscapes.

And North America has great landscapes in abundance. They inspired awe in the original inhabitants and often something close to disbelief in later travellers, nowhere more so than the Grand Canyon. This is a dead cert on any list of Seven Natural Wonders of the World. Its desert-bared, rainbow-coloured rocks are like a condensed geological history ranging back half a billion years.

The landscapes of California's Sierra Nevada and especially Yosemite Valley have also inspired awe in millions. Their unique place in the history of conservation and of the earth sciences is largely due to one man, John Muir. Muir's Yosemite studies helped establish a true understanding of the major sculptural force of glaciers, and he is also widely revered as the progenitor of today's conservation movements. Muir was – of course – also a great walker.

In Wyoming's Teton Range, sky-stabbing peaks are mirrored in crystalline glacial lakes. It's a complex landscape; forests, rivers, wetlands and glaciers are all part of the mosaic. The climate is sometimes harsh but summers are short and intense, splashing the valleys with brilliant displays of flowers.

In the Canadian Rockies lies another site of prime importance to the earth sciences; the Burgess Shales, formed in a shallow sea and now raised 2,250 m (7,400 ft) above sea level, represent the richest single source of information about early life on Earth. Though marvellous to contemplate, this is not a wonder that can be grasped at a glance, for it lies amid some of the finest scenery in the Rocky Mountains.

Far to the east in Newfoundland, the tablelands and fjords of Gros Morne National Park also have huge significance for our understanding of the earth. Its rich geological mix includes rocks rarely found at the surface, giving an insight into the nature of the planet's interior.

If some sites open a window into the distant past, Hawaii is all about geology happening right now. This is nicely underlined by the fact that hiking trails can occasionally be closed because of volcanic activity. Images of American landscape may be spread around the world, but there's no danger of anticlimax; the reality is too grand.

OVERLEAF *Moulton Barn, Grand Teton National Park, Wyoming*

▽ *Glacier Point, Yosemite Valley, Sierra Nevada*

SIERRA NEVADA
The Range of Light

ROLY SMITH

It was on a glowing April day in 1868 that the 29-year-old John Muir, fresh from his epic 1,000-mile walk through post-Civil War America from his home in Indiana to the Gulf of Mexico, first set eyes on the Sierra Nevada.

Landing in bustling, cosmopolitan San Francisco after taking a steamship from snow-bound New York, he is said to have stopped someone in the street and asked: 'What's the quickest way out of town?'

'Where do you want to go?' was the reply.

'To any place that is wild,' said Muir.

Thus fate directed him towards Yosemite and the Sierra Nevada, which was to become his spiritual home and the constant inspiration for his pioneering nature writing and conservation campaigning for 46 years. Passing through the fertile Central Valley of California, he climbed to the crest of the Coast Range at Pacheco Pass. Before him lay the San Joaquin valley, then uncultivated and glowing gold with wild arnica flowers, and beyond that, the purple-footed, snow-capped Sierra Nevada.

Muir wrote of the mighty Sierra rising 'miles in height, reposing like a smooth, cumulous cloud in the sunny sky, and so gloriously colored, and so luminous, it seems to be not clothed in light, but wholly composed of it, like the wall of some celestial city... Then it seemed to me the Sierra should be called not the Nevada, or Snowy Range, but the Range of Light.'

Anyone who has had the joy of walking through the range would heartily agree. It is not surprising that some of America's finest mountain photographers, from Ansel Adams to Galen Rowell, also made their homes here, vividly portraying that perfect, translucent light.

▽ *Looking east over Half Dome*

DESCRIPTION: the John Muir Trail (JMT) is a serious, 220-mile mountain backpacking trip, but you can get a good taste of it by trying some of the day walks suggested

LOCATION: central Sierra Nevada of California, USA

WHEN TO GO: if you want to avoid snow in the high passes, mid-July to late August

JMT START: Happy Isles, Yosemite Valley

JMT FINISH: Whitney Portal, west of Lone Pine

DURATION: usually takes between a fortnight and a month to complete in one trip, although as stated, many people do it in stages/day walks

MAXIMUM ALTITUDE: Mt Whitney, 4,418 m (14,494 ft)

ACCOMMODATION: plentiful accommodation accessible from various trailheads along the way, such as Mammoth Lakes, Red's Meadow, Vermillion Valley, Silver Lake or Bishop

SPECIAL CONSIDERATIONS: if you are doing anything more than a day hike, you'll need to carry all your food with you or re-supply at pre-planned points, such as Mammoth Lakes or Bishop

PERMITS/RESTRICTIONS: permits required for JMT, available from the Wilderness Management Offices of the Yosemite and Sequoia-King's Canyon National Parks

GUIDEBOOK: *Guide to the John Muir* Trail by Thomas Winnett and Kathy Morey, pb Wilderness Press

By far the best way of enjoying the Sierra Nevada is on foot, and best of all is to follow the 220-mile John Muir Trail, from Yosemite National Park to Mount Whitney, at 4,418 m (14,494 ft) the highest point in the contiguous United States – and an optional mountaineering ascent. As a continuous hike it's a serious backpacking adventure, but many people do it in sections and much of it is within a day's hike from a trailhead.

The spirit of Muir and the Sierra is epitomized in the dizzily-soaring granite walls, tumbling waterfalls and giant sequoia redwoods of Yosemite. Once you escape the choking traffic in the valley floor (why can't they close it and allow just buses or bikes?) and get out into the back country, you begin to realise what captivated Muir, Adams and countless other artists and photographers.

Summit baggers will relish the 26 km (16 mile) day hike up the back side of 2,695 m (8,842 ft) Half Dome, the climax of which involves hauling yourself up exposed wire cables bolted to the granite. Much more satisfying is the 9.5 km (6 mile) Vernal Falls-Nevada Falls

Loop, which follows the Mist Trail to Vernal Falls and returns by the John Muir Trail via Clark Point and the plummeting Nevada Falls under the towering dome of Liberty Cap.

△ Tuolumne Meadows

If you want the pleasure without the pain (except in your knees, that is), descend the 7.4 km (4.6 mile) Four-Mile Trail from Glacier Point, perhaps the most famous of the Yosemite viewpoints, to the valley floor. Its seemingly endless, jarring, switchbacks reveal ever-changing views of the valley.

The JMT leaves Yosemite via the alpine Tuolumne Meadows and then goes through the Ansel Adams and John Muir Wilderness areas, passing a succession of beautiful lakes and tarns beneath towering granite peaks. A real wilderness trek, it scarcely ever descends below 2,740 m (9,000 ft) and is uncrossed by any roads for 225 km (140 miles) between Tioga Pass in the north and Sherman Pass in the south.

But your reward will be to find out, as John Muir did: 'I only went out for a walk, and finally concluded to stay out till sundown, for going out, I found, was really going in.'

◁◁ Sequoia redwoods

GRAND TETONS
The Grand Teton Loop

CAMERON M. BURNS

▽ *Yellowstone Falls, a favourite Yellowstone/ Tetons tourist spot*

On U.S. 89 between Moose and Moran Junction, Wyoming, is the spot where one of the world's most famous photographs was taken. In 1942, Ansel Adams unpacked his camera equipment, set up his tripod, and – just before sunset – snapped an iconic image of the Teton Range that would come to symbolize not just the Tetons but the American West itself.

But for the walker the image is something of a deception. It's taken from the plains, from the side of the road – from civilization. It's nice for posters and greeting cards, but to know the real Tetons one must immerse oneself in the range.

Luckily, there are many fine opportunities, including the Grand Teton Loop, a combination of several well-established trails within the park (Cascade Canyon, Teton Crest Trail, Death Canyon, Valley Trail, etc.), as well as the individual walks themselves.

Ironically, the Grand Teton Loop (and the Cascade Canyon Trail) starts out on a boat. At the Jenny Lake Boat Dock and visitors' center, you catch a ferry across the lake. You'll be in awe as the sharply pointed peaks of Mounts Owen and Teewinot, and Mount St John loom up ever higher, towering like gothic cathedrals above the water (as a young climber, I once paddled a dead log across this lake because I couldn't afford the ferry – I recommend paying for the ticket).

At the far side, past hordes of tourists gawking at Hidden Falls and milling around Inspiration Point, the walk begins. The trail up Cascade Canyon starts out rather steeply and remains so for the first 1.5 km (1 mile). Then it flattens out considerably and you see that Cascade Canyon literally splits the range. After about 8 km (5 miles), the trail splits, and the South Fork of the Cascade Canyon Trail heads off to the southwest. Day-walkers will probably want to turn back here; it's 8 km (5 miles) to the split; 16 km (10 miles) round-trip. To continue with the Grand Teton Loop, look for a place to camp about 3 km (2 miles) after the split; there is one fairly established campsite.

△ *One of the many streams draining Grand Teton National Park*

facts and figures

DESCRIPTION: spectacular day walks, with the prospect of a four-day backpacking loop, through very rugged Rocky Mountain high country

LOCATION: northwestern Wyoming, in the United States' northern Rocky Mountains

WHEN TO GO: August and September. Even July can see deep snow

START/FINISH: South Jenny Lake Trailhead

DURATION: the walks take from half a day to four (long) days.

MAX ALTITUDE: 3,288 m (10,788 ft).

ACCOMMODATION: tents only on the Loop. Wide range of local options (cabins, B&Bs, luxury hotel rooms, etc.) for the day walks

SPECIAL CONSIDERATIONS: this is bear country – so be prepared: avoid hiking at night, hang food when camping, avoid running (you can surprise a bear), and get away from carcasses quickly. Pepper spray is a good idea. Also, trekking poles are helpful crossing old snow banks. And remember, fierce, winter weather can engulf you in any season

PERMITS/RESTRICTIONS: backcountry permits are required for overnight stops in Grand Teton National Park. They are available at visitor centers at Moose and Colter Bay, and at the Jenny Lake Ranger Station. For more information, call the park at 307 739 3309. Also, to complete this loop requires a ferry ride to the start of Cascade Canyon. For more information, see www.jennylakeboating.com

GUIDEBOOK: *Hiking Grand Teton National Park* (2nd ed) by Bill Schneider, Falcon/Globe Pequot.

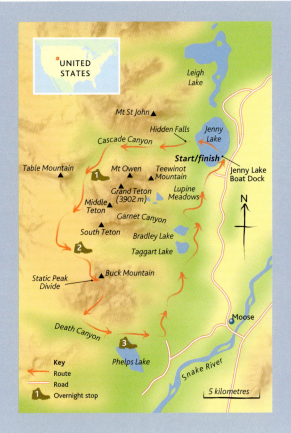

Days two and three of the Loop circle widely around Mount Owen, the Grand, Middle and South Tetons, and then Buck Mountain. The route crests three passes, Hurricane Pass, Buck Mountain Pass, and Static Peak Divide, narrowly the highest at 3,288 m (10,788 ft). The walk then begins a huge descent, switchbacking continuously down Death Canyon. Phelps Lake is the next overnight stop.

The last day of the Loop is a bit of a marathon as the trail meanders over moraines and through mature forests with abundant wildlife. It continues past Taggart and Bradley Lakes and eventually joins the spectacular Garnet Canyon Trail, before dropping down to Lupine Meadows, from where you can walk, or try to hitch, 1.5 km (1 mile) back to the South Jenny Lake Trailhead.

Lupine Meadows is also the starting point for the Garnet Canyon Trail. It's a 6.5 km (4 miles) hike venturing into the world of the hardcore mountaineers who are there to climb the Grand. Initially the trail wanders through mature Northern Rockies forests before making a long right-hander and heading straight up towards the peaks. The trail begins a series of many switchbacks as it climbs steeply toward the head of the canyon and the picturesque Middle Teton. The clanking of climbing equipment and the tightly stuffed packs of technical mountaineers become a common sight. The trail eventually peters out into climbers' tracks, which you can follow as far as you feel like.

The Loop and its sub-components – like the Cascade and Garnet Canyon Trails – are fabulous high-country walks with the opportunity to create many pictures just as iconic as Adams' 1942 photo – even better, in fact, as you can put yourself inside that famed image.

△ *Classic view of the Tetons from the southeast*

THE GRAND CANYON
A Journey to the Birth of the Earth

ROLY SMITH

A Texas cowpoke had just taken a job with an Arizona outfit that ran its stock on the Kaibab Plateau, not far from the South Rim of the Grand Canyon. Trouble was, no one had told him about the canyon, and one day when he was rounding up some strays he suddenly found himself staring into the yawning abyss.

His jaw dropped, he took off his hat, wiped the sweat from his forehead and exclaimed: 'My God! Something has happened here!'

▽ *On the Bright Angel Trail*

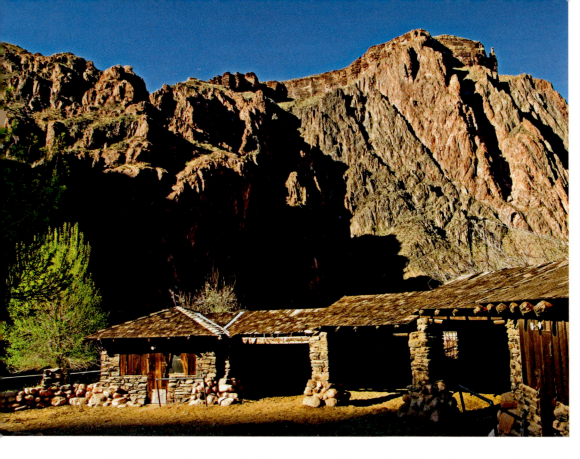

◁ *Stables at Phantom Ranch*

The story may be apocryphal but most people react similarly on first seeing the Grand Canyon. 'Awesome' is a much overused word, especially in the States, but for once it is the only adjective which comes close to describing this 1,500 m (5,000 ft) deep, 16 km (10 miles) wide chasm. which slices through the Colorado plateau for over 430 km (270 miles). It reveals 570 million years of the Earth's history.

Most visitors are content just to stop and stare as the ever-changing light brings the mesas, buttes and cliff faces into a constant kaleidoscope of colours. But braver souls will want to explore the hidden depths to discover the agent behind this natural masterpiece – the thing that made the Grand Canyon 'happen' – the swirling, sediment-filled waters of the mighty Colorado River, now harnessed by the massive Glen Canyon Dam impounding Lake Powell 24 km (15 miles) upstream.

Lake Powell commemorates the astonishing Civil War veteran John Wesley Powell, who in 1869, having lost his right arm at the Battle of Shiloh, led a crew of nine men and four boats on the first descent of the Colorado canyon by boat. Their aim was to chart the last great unmapped white space on the map of the American west, and after 95 days of danger and adventure, they succeeded.

Now many of the Park's five million annual tourists can enjoy safe, sanitized whitewater excursions through the gorge, take helicopter flights above it, or hitch a ride on

△ View of the Grand Canyon from the South Rim

one of the rather malodorous mule trains which ply in and out. There is also the unfortunate new 'Skywalk' on the Hualapai Indian Reservation, which juts out 21 m (70 ft) from the South Rim, 1,220 m (4,000 ft) above the river. But really, the only way to appreciate the sheer scale of the canyon is to descend to the river on foot.

Most hikers will plump for one of the many engineered trails which descend from the far busier (and lower) South Rim or the quieter and higher North Rim, returning the way they came. But if you are really fit and ambitious and have booked return transport and overnight accommodation at Phantom Ranch, you might want to combine the Bright Angel Trail with one of the two steeper Kaibab Trails and hike out to the other side.

The easiest walk to reach the river is to follow the mules on the Bright Angel Trail from the South Rim. Initially, it switchbacks down through gnarled pinyons and junipers, past white limestone cliffs before it drops steeply through formations of red, purple and tan Supai sandstones to reach the Red Wall and green Bright Angel shales. The oasis of Indian

facts and figures

DESCRIPTION: a strenuous 18-mile (up and down) day hike. An overnight camp or stay at Phantom Ranch is recommended

LOCATION: Kaibab Plateau, Arizona, USA

WHEN TO GO: spring or autumn are the best times to avoid baking temperatures in the inner canyon

START/FINISH: Bright Angel Trailhead, Kolb Studio, South Rim

DURATION: 4–5 hours down, 5–7 hours up

MAXIMUM ALTITUDE: Bright Angel Trailhead, South Rim: 2,091 m (6,860 ft)

ACCOMMODATION: lodging and campsites are plentiful on both South and North Rims and at Phantom Ranch: all need to be booked well in advance

SPECIAL CONSIDERATIONS: carry at least four litres (one gallon) of water per person, per day. Be prepared for temperatures of up to 48°C (120 °F) in the inner canyon in summer, with little shade

PERMITS/RESTRICTIONS: you'll need a wilderness permit from the Grand Canyon National Park to stay overnight

GUIDEBOOKS: *The Grand Canyon and the American South West* by Constance Roos, pb Cicerone Press; *Grand Canyon Handbook* by Bill Weir, pb Moon Travel Handbooks, Avalon Travel Publishing

Springs, with its cottonwood trees and tumbling waterfalls, comes as a welcome relief. Plunging down now to cross the Tonto Platform, you are at the 500 million-year-old geological level, and the final trek to the river is short, steep and usually very hot. At long last the churning, boiling river comes into view, and the pleasures of the idyllically-situated Phantom Ranch, embowered in cottonwoods, await you over the suspension bridge.

Your journey is complete. All you have to do now is walk up out of this incredible, upside down, inside out mountain which has taken you back in geological time to the virtual birth of the Earth.

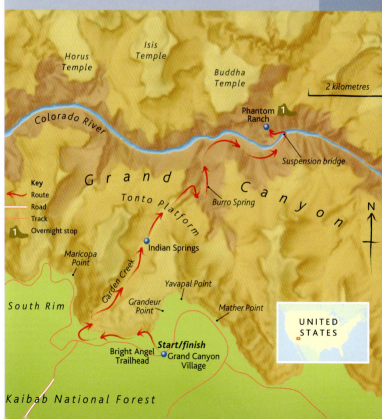

HAWAII
Volcanoes National Park

JON SPARKS

△ *Lava Waterfall flowing
into the Pacific Ocean*

Superlatives cluster around Hawaii. Further from other land than almost anywhere else on earth, it can also claim the world's tallest mountain. Mauna Kea may be a relatively modest 4,205 m (13,796 ft) above sea level, but rises about 10,200 m (33,500 ft) from the ocean floor. Hawaii is also home to the most consistently active volcanic area on the planet.

Hawaii is the name of a US state, of an archipelago and also of the largest island; to avoid confusion this is frequently called the Big Island. The archipelago, strung out over 600 km (375 miles), tracks the movement of the Pacific crustal plate over a 'hot-spot' or convection plume in the Earth's mantle. The Big Island is the youngest and is still growing, with lava-flows regularly reshaping the landscape, often flowing into the sea amid vast clouds of steam. Its geographic isolation also means that there are many unique species of flora and fauna, which colonise the fresh ground as it cools.

Hawaii's Volcanoes National Park encompasses both 1,250 m (4,101 ft) Kilauea and 4,170 m (13,682 ft) Mauna Loa (also notable as the site of some of the world's leading astronomical observatories). Since the foundation of the Hawaiian Volcano Observatory in 1911 they have been intensively studied, but there is still much to learn and it remains impossible to predict eruptions with certainty. Anyone planning a visit needs to be prepared for possible disruption. Regular updates also guide those who want to see active lava flows.

Kilauea has been continuously active since 1983, with almost all episodes centred on the Pu 'u 'O 'o crater, best viewed at a discreet distance. Fortunately there is much to explore around the mountain's other craters and vents, which are by no means inert.

Kilauea's main caldera is encircled by the Crater Rim Trail, a loop of about 18 km (11 miles). The ground is often rough and with so much to see it's wise to allow a full day. The surroundings vary from the desert-like bareness of recent lava flows to carpets of luxuriant ferns and forest. The weather can be equally variable, with strong winds and heavy rain apt to sweep in from the Pacific with little warning.

After viewing the crater from above on the Crater Rim Trail, it can be seen at ground level from the Halema'uma'u Trail. Look out for the contorted forms of pahoehoe lava flows and be prepared for sulphurous fumes in the Halema'uma'u crater itself. (People with respiratory ailments are officially advised to avoid this trail.) The Halema'uma'u Trail can be taken as a one-way trip of 5.6 km (3.5 miles), or a varied return made by the Byron Ledge Trail, with its elevated views of the main caldera.

Strong walkers could further combine this with the Kilauea Iki Trail, which can also be taken on its own. It's a 6.5 km (4 mile) loop which begins by descending 120 m (400 ft)

▽ *Steam rising from the rim of the Halema'uma'u crater*

DESCRIPTION: exciting and sometimes rough day-walks in active volcanic terrain; tough backpacking options also available

LOCATION: south-eastern side of the island of Hawaii

WHEN TO GO: year-round; September and October are usually the driest (or least wet) months

START: most walks start from Kilauea Visitor Centre, close to the crater rim

DURATION: half- to full-day walks on Kilauea; 3–4 days for ascent of Mauna Loa

MAX ALTITUDE: 1,250 m (4,101 ft) on Kilauea; 4,170 m (13,682 ft) on Mauna Loa

ACCOMMODATION: campgrounds and Volcano House Hotel on Kilauea; basic mountain huts on Mauna Loa

SPECIAL CONSIDERATIONS/EQUIPMENT NEEDED: be prepared for widely variable weather, with snow always possible on Mauna Loa. Check for latest eruption information at http://volcano.wr.usgs.gov/hvostatus.php

PERMITS/RESTRICTIONS: no wild camping. Permits required for Napau Trail and Mauna Loa

GUIDEBOOK: *Lonely Planet Hiking in Hawaii* by Sara Benson and Jennifer Snarski

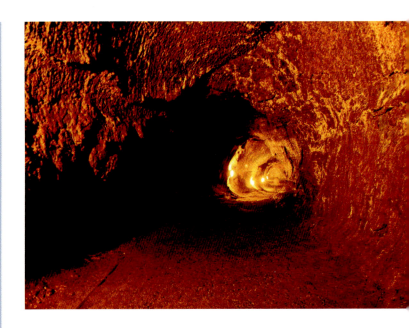

through lush rain forest. The lava flows of the crater floor date from the 1959 eruption and still generate billows of steam. The Trail's eastern end is at a parking area which also serves the remarkable Thurston Lava Tube, formed when the outer surface of a stream of lava solidified but molten rock continued to drain through the interior.

◁ ◁ *Thurston Lava Tube*

The closest approach to currently active areas is the Napau Trail, a 22 km (14 mile) loop. Because of the active state of the eruption, even day-hikers are required to register for this one.

For a different, and altogether more rigorous experience, there's the ascent of mighty Mauna Loa. Overall gradients are gentle but the lava slopes are incredibly rough. Other challenges include the altitude, the highly changeable and sometimes extreme weather, and the lack of surface water. For all these reasons progress is usually much slower than mere distance would suggest. Allow 3–4 days. (It might appear possible to reach the summit and return in a day from the end of the Observatory Road, but it's not recommended. This route is also less varied and geologically striking.) There are huts for the overnight stops, with mattresses, toilets and rain-water tanks, but otherwise you'll need to be self-sufficient.

▽ *Pu 'u 'O 'o crater*

NEWFOUNDLAND
Gros Morne National Park

JON SPARKS

Western Newfoundland, and Gros Morne National Park in particular, has played a key role in the development of the theory of plate tectonics, which now guides our understanding of the processes that built the earth's crust. Sometimes called 'The Galapagos of Geology', Gros Morne's mix of rocks is exposed in a spectacular landscape of glaciated fjords and cliffs. Its coastal lowlands and arctic plateau reveal a diverse tapestry of habitats.

Two short introductory trails start near the Park's Discovery Centre. The 5 km (3.1 mile) Lookout Trail is steep, although provided with boardwalks and steps, climbing through

▽ *Herd of caribou*

forest to damp meadows and bare plateau. The summit of Partridgeberry Hill gives a 360-degree view over the forked fjords of Bonne Bay and up to the Long Range mountains.

The shorter and easier Tablelands Trail visits probably the prime geological site in the Park. The Tablelands are composed of peridotite, originating deep in the Earth's mantle, which was driven to the surface by the collision of tectonic plates. Peridotite is deficient in plant nutrients such as calcium, and contains large amounts of toxic heavy metals, explaining the bleak, almost desert-like bareness of much of the ground.

Further along Route 431 is the Wallace Brook trailhead, starting point for the Green Gardens Trail, which descends from the plateau to a fretted coast of stacks and cliffs, often topped with flower-rich meadows. Sheltered coves, frequently deserted, lie below. The full trail is 16 km (10 miles) long and rough in places; it's also necessary to ford Wallace Book, which can be tricky after heavy rain.

A contrasting coastal trail lies further north at Green Point, a 3 km (1.9 mile) (one way) stroll along an old mail road hugging a low-lying shoreline. The long stony beach is backed by small ponds and patches of tuckamore. Tuckamore forest is a phenomenon of exposed coasts; in the salt-laden winds trees grow only to leeward, developing low, contorted forms.

▽ *Sunset at Bonne Bay*

Further north again is the Western Brook Pond Trail, a moderate 3 km (1.9 mile) (one way). 'Pond' is an inadequate word for this 30 km (18.6 mile) ribbon lake, its upper reaches confined by towering cliffs. Glacier-scoured, it was once a fjord, but as the land rose, rebounding from the pressure of the ice, it was cut off from the sea. The highest waterfall in eastern North America tumbles into the Pond, rejoicing in the name of Pissing Mare Falls. During the summer season boat trips are available, and there's also a continuation trail – a further 5 km (3.1 miles) (one way) to the fine beach of Snug Harbour near the narrowing of the lake.

The *piece de resistance* among day walks here is the ascent of Gros Morne Mountain, at 806 m (2,644 ft) the highest in the park and second highest in Newfoundland. The James Callaghan Trail – named for the former British Prime Minister, an ardent conservationist – is a tough 16 km (10 mile) route which needs a full day. The upper section is usually closed in early season but the first half can still be done; this is a fairly gentle ascent to a clutch of pools below the upper slopes.

△ Ptarmigan

facts and figures

DESCRIPTION: day walks along rugged coast and spectacular glaciated uplands

LOCATION: Gros Morne National Park in western Newfoundland, Canada

WHEN TO GO: the Park is open year-round but the main season is from mid-May to early October. The James Callaghan Trail is typically closed until early July

START/FINISH: various points along Highway 430 (bus service) and near the National Park Discovery Centre

DURATION: from 2 hours to full day hikes

MAX ALTITUDE: 806 m (2,644 ft)

ACCOMMODATION: campgrounds within the park, range of accommodation at Deer Lake, 32 km (20 miles) from the Park entrance.

SPECIAL CONSIDERATIONS/EQUIPMENT NEEDED: be prepared for Arctic weather on mountain routes at any time of year

PERMITS/RESTRICTIONS: National Park Entry fees for all visitors. Back-country hiking and camping fees, registration and briefing for those tackling multi-day routes

GUIDEBOOK: *Newfoundland & Labrador* by Andrew Hempstead, pb Frommer's

From here a steep climb up a bouldery gully gains the summit plateau. This exposed landscape feels bleak even in summer. It's really a slice of Arctic tundra, the stony ground thinly carpeted with low, tenacious vegetation. The area is home to caribou, Arctic hare and rock ptarmigan. Hikers should stick to the marked path to avoid disturbing the habitat. The route then descends the north-eastern slopes and loops back to the north of the peak to rejoin the outward route.

There is back-country campsite accomodation at the far point of the route for those who'd like to spend a night in the wilderness. Facilities are limited to a pit toilet and the ever-present and essential bear pole (to keep food supplies out of reach of hungry bears), so hikers need to be self-sufficient. The same is true for the longer hiking trails in the park, for which walkers must attend a mandatory briefing and demonstrate navigational proficiency. Hikers are also required to carry a VHF beacon. Clearly this is real back-country, but the preparations are well worth the effort to experience a genuine slice of Canadian wilderness.

▽ *Western Brook Pond*

BRITISH COLUMBIA
The Burgess Highline Trail, Yoho National Park

ROLY SMITH

▷▷ *Summit of the Vice President, as seen from the Highline Trail*

▽ *The Takakkaw Falls, seen at the start of the walk*

An insignificant shale quarry on the barren slopes of the aptly-named Fossil Ridge between the towering crags of Mount Wapta and Mount Field in Yoho National Park in the Canadian Rockies can lay claim to be one of the earth's greatest natural wonders.

This World Heritage Site – which can only be visited as part of a pre-booked, guided party, with strictly no souvenir samples allowed – is the place where self-taught geologist Charles Doolittle Walcott first discovered tiny fossils of strange creatures which lived in an ancient sea a mind-boggling 540 million years ago. They represented the very dawn of life on earth.

The Burgess Highline Trail, a strenuous day hike from the Yoho Valley across the Yoho and Burgess Passes and back into Field, runs just beneath Walcott's famous quarry. It also affords some of the best mountain walking through the heart of the Rockies, and what the distinguished palaeontologist Stephen Jay Gould called: 'one of the finest sights on our continent.'

Almost everything about Yoho is superlative; the First Nation settlers of the Cree tribe, who made their home here, seem to have thought so too. The Cree word 'Yoho' literally means 'Wow!' while the name of the Takakkaw Falls, at the start of our walk, translates as 'It is magnificent!'

The falls, thought to be the highest unbroken waterfall in Canada, are fed by the meltwaters of the Daly Glacier and Waputik Icefield and tumble 380 m (1,250 ft) in a thundering plume of spray. They make a spectacular and memorable start to your walk, which heads down the road towards the Whiskey Jack Hostel and trailhead, named after the old miners' nickname for the gray, or Canada, jay.

Entering the forest now, with enticing glimpses of the Takakkaw Falls and the Waputik Icefield through the pines, a series of switchbacks gains height rapidly, towards Yoho Lake. This tree-skirted tarn, where there is backcountry camping, has superb views of the glaciated north face of Mount Victoria.

It is a short step from here, past a sign (nibbled by hungry porcupines) which prohibits further unguided access towards the site of the Burgess Shales, to the Yoho Pass. You traverse an exposed scree slope enlivened by the alarm whistles of curious hoary marmots, beneath a towering wall of rock, getting a glimpse of the usually invisible No-see-um Falls, tumbling off the snowfields of the President Range.

You eventually emerge from the forest onto exposed mountainside beneath the vertical crags of Wapta Mountain, 2,778 m (9,116 ft), with increasingly fine views of Mount Burgess, 2,559 m (8,525 ft) ahead and Emerald Lake, glinting with facets like the jewel from which it gets its name, embowered in trees 900 m (3,000 ft) below. To the north, the

facts and figures

DESCRIPTION: a strenuous 21 km (13 mile) all-day hike through forest and across exposed mountainsides

LOCATION: Yoho National Park, British Columbia, Canada

WHEN TO GO: July to September

START: Takakkaw Falls Trailhead, Yoho Valley, British Columbia

FINISH: Field, off Highway 1A, British Columbia

DURATION: full day hike of 7–9 hours

MAXIMUM ALTITUDE: Fossil Ridge: c 2,225 m (c 7,300 ft)

ACCOMMODATION: there is a hostel at Whiskey Jack, near Takakkaw Falls, a campsite at Takakkaw Falls, and plenty of accommodation in Field

SPECIAL CONSIDERATIONS/EQUIPMENT: this is a hard day in the mountains, so you will need to be equipped for any sudden changes in the weather

PERMITS/RESTRICTIONS: access to Walcott Quarry is severely restricted, and if you want to visit you will need a special permit or be booked into a guided party arranged through the National Park Information Centre at Field or the Yoho Burgess Shale Foundation

GUIDEBOOKS: *The Wonder of Yoho* by Don Beers, pb Rocky Mountain Books; *The Canadian Rockies Access Guide* by John Dodd and Gail Helgasson, pb Lone Pine Publishing; *Wonderful Life:The Burgess Shale and the Nature of History* by Stephen Jay Gould, pb W W Norton

virgin snow fields and glaciers of the President and Vice President glisten in the sun, and to the south the mighty ramparts of Burgess defend our destination of Field and the Kicking Horse Pass.

Passing through low scrub, the Burgess Shale Quarry is seen high on your left as you traverse a good path beneath the ridge, heading for the col between Mount Field and Mount Burgess to eventually reach the crest of Burgess Pass at around 2,200 m (7,218 ft). Now begins the long 8.2 km (5.1 mile) and tortuous, two-hour descent via a knee-jarring, seemingly never-ending series of 48 switchbacks (yes, I counted them) to the Kicking Horse Pass, with the jagged spires of Mount Stephen ahead, dominating the Canadian Pacific Railway town of Field.

The interminable switchbacks lead you back into the forest, finally reaching the roaring roadside of the Trans-Canada Highway. From here it is a 1.3 km (0.8 mile) walk along the busy highway to complete your journey from the origins of life on earth back to civilisation at Field.

◁◁ *Looking back to Mt Wtapa from the trail*

▽ *View of Emerald Lake, as seen from Highline Trail*

SOUTH AMERICA

"The health of the eye seems to demand a horizon.
We are never tired, so long as we can see far enough."

RALPH WALDO EMERSON

△ *Torres del Paine,*
Patagonia, Chile

The geography of South America is dominated by two magnificent phenomena; the world's longest mountain range and its greatest river. There is some disagreement whether the Amazon or the Nile is the world's longest river but the Amazon drains by far the largest basin, and carries the largest volume of water – a fifth of all the fresh water that flows into the world's oceans. The Amazon basin accounts for 40 per cent of the continent's land area, and most of this, despite habitat loss, is still lush rainforest.

Though dwarfed by Amazonia, Brazil's Mata Atlântica, or Atlantic Forest, is a hugely important ecological region. Large tracts have been cleared and serious threats remain, but significant areas are now protected. Its shoreline, the Discovery Coast, is now a UNESCO World Heritage site, and home to some of the finest beaches on the planet.

There's no challenge to the Andes as the world's longest mountain range; at around 7,200 km (4,500 m) they're almost twice the length of the Himalaya. Near their farthest southern extremity are the Cordillera del Paine, in Chilean Patagonia. The Torres del Paine are among the most precipitous peaks in the world, one of the great theatres of Big Wall climbing. The Paine region is only about 50 degrees south of the Equator, but climatically it feels sub-Arctic. The region is notorious for high winds. This can make life tough for the walker, but ultimately it only adds to the drama of this extraordinary landscape.

It's generally accepted that the Andes are lower than the Himalaya, with the highest peaks falling just short of 7,000 m (22,966 ft), but the question of altitude is more complicated than it appears. The earth is not a perfect sphere, and in fact the point furthest from its centre – the point, if you like, where you could be closest to the moon – is not the summit of Everest but that of Chimborazo in Ecuador. Conventionally measured at 6,267 m (20,561 ft), Chimborazo is an axe-and-crampons climb, albeit a relatively straightforward one, and so falls outside the scope of this book. However, not too far away is Sangay, also riding high on the Earth's equatorial bulge. Sangay is an active volcano, and its awesome views stretch from Chimborazo in the west to valleys far below which feed the Amazon.

Further north, in Venezuela, are the extraordinary tepuis; flat-topped mountains rimmed by great cliffs, thrusting almost violently from the rolling savannahs and forests. These eroded remnants of a once vast sandstone plateau are ecological islands, home to many unique species. Their isolation and mystery make them exceptionally provocative to fertile imaginations and many myths, legends and modern fictions have germinated here.

It's true everywhere; a few walks cannot encapsulate a continent. But then again, there's no better way to begin to get the measure of South America.

OVERLEAF *Mount Roraima, Venezuela*

▽ *Mount Chimborazo, Ecuador*

ECUADOR
Sangay National Park

JON SPARKS

Ecuador may be the smallest of the Andean nations, but it packs an awful lot in. In particular, it has some of the world's highest active volcanoes as well as Chimborazo, with its claim to be the highest mountain on Earth. The choice of walking and trekking is all but inexhaustible and picking just one itinerary is fraught, but the suggested route offers a bit of everything, from rainforest to glacier.

▽ *Tungarahua volcano*

It culminates in a close encounter with, and possible climb of, Sangay, generally considered the world's highest active volcano, reaching 5,230 m (17,160 ft) by the conventional yardstick. Sangay is not part of the main cordillera ranges but rises more than 4,500 m (15,000 ft) above deep valleys (which feed the Amazon Basin); this extreme altitude range gives Sangay National Park a stunning diversity of climates and ecosystems.

You may feel the altitude even before the trek starts, as the normal port of entry is Quito, one of the highest capitals in the world at 2,850 m (9,350 ft). It's certainly wise to spend some time acclimatizing before attempting Sangay. From Quito the approach follows the fertile central valley known as the Avenue of the Volcanoes – beat that for a stirring name!

△ *El Altar*

The trekking route starts near the village of Candelleria at the entrance to the Park and soon leaves cultivated land, climbing gradually to dramatic views of El Altar. This is a jagged, broken ring of peaks surrounding a crater around 3 km (1.9 miles) across, left by a cataclysmic eruption. The peaks are are among the most technically demanding rock and ice climbs in Ecuador. The amazing spectacle just gets bigger and better on the easy walk to the meadows of Collanes at the entrance to the crater.

The following day begins with a climb to 4,550 m (14,929 ft) to cross a flanking ridge. There are stunning views of El Altar and the volcanic cone of Tungarahua and, in the distance, mighty Chimborazo. A rough descent brings you to Laguna Mandur, a narrow glacier-fed lake flanked by black lava. The night's camp is beside Laguna Estrellada.

The third day is a long steady walk, without major climbs or descents, across wide high moorland (known as *paramo*) dotted with numerous lakes; in calm weather they make perfect mirrors for the surrounding peaks. Four days are spent crossing watersheds and following valleys, often through montane forest, to reach the base of Sangay and the area of La Playa. This of course means 'beach', though it's over 200 km (125 miles) from the sea and around 3,600 m (11,800 ft) above it. Yet there is something vaguely beach-like about this great sprawl of gritty red lava.

Sangay looms over the camp; its activity can often be heard and may be seen as a glow in the sky at night. It has been relatively quiet in the last few years, though by no means

▷ *Indian farms at the edge of Sangay National Park*

facts and figures

DESCRIPTION: tough trekking over high passes and plateaus and through deep river valleys, with possible ascent of high active volcano

LOCATION: Sangay national park, in south-eastern Ecuador

WHEN TO GO: year round

START: town of Riobamba, accessible by bus from Quito

FINISH: town of Banos

DURATION: as described, 11 days trekking. Shorter variants are possible, with a 2- or 3- day trek to El Altar especially popular

MAX ALTITUDE: 5,230 m (17,160 ft) at summit of Sangay; about 4,550 m (14,930 ft) for those opting out of the climb

ACCOMMODATION: wild camping with full porter support

SPECIAL CONSIDERATIONS/EQUIPMENT NEEDED: this trek spends considerable time above 4,000 m (13,125 ft), with consequent risk of altitude sickness. Crampons may be required for the final stages of the Sangay ascent

PERMITS/RESTRICTIONS: entry fee to Sangay National Park

GUIDEBOOK: *Climbing & Hiking in Ecuador* by Rob Rachowiecki & Mark Thurber, pb Bradt Travel Guides

dormant, and could flare up with little warning. Sangay is a classic stratovolcano, a layered cone of lava, ash and pyroclastic material. It's in the same class as Ngauruhoe and Etna, which appear elsewhere in this volume and also, more worryingly, as Mt St Helens. Despite its height there's no permanent snow or ice at the top because of the heat.

Weather and volcanic activity permitting, the ascent of the peak starts before dawn. The climb presents no technical difficulties, just a long slog up slopes of scree and scoria, and probably snow near the top. The main challenge is the altitude; it's vital to go slowly and to monitor yourself and others for signs of altitude sickness. The top sports three craters, but two show only low-level activity with steam and gases issuing from vents. It's the easternmost crater which is currently most active, and the eastern rim which provides the awesome prospect towards the Amazon basin around 5,000 m (16,500 ft) below.

After the ascent the final days of trekking are a great contrast, across another high plateau and pass, then down the Pucara valley to the village of Elen. It's common to transfer from here to the spa town of Banos, where the hot pools are ideal for easing tired muscles.

▽ *Sangay volcano*

BRAZIL
The Discovery Coast

JON SPARKS

While hard walks bring their own reward, and give the measure of hard places, there's nothing wrong with taking it a little easy now and then. And where better for a relaxed few days' hiking than a beach?

Not just any beach, either. Brazil's Discovery Coast serves up a succession of beaches as good as any in the world, with dazzling white sands backed by terracotta cliffs, looking out to the turquoise infinity of the Atlantic. For much of its length the beach is fringed by offshore reefs, sheltering calm, warm inshore water. There are accessible and popular spots with beach bars and sunbathers, but long stretches are virtually deserted, like the beach of dreams.

▽ *Beach at Trancoso*

The Discovery Coast is the seaboard of the Mata Atlântica (Portuguese for Atlantic Forest) a region of unexcelled biodiversity designated a World Biosphere Reserve. Really we should speak of Atlantic *Forests,* as there are various distinct types. Though large tracts have been lost, the remainder still houses an incredible reservoir of life, with a greater variety of primate life, for example, than anywhere else on earth. Researchers are said to have counted over 450 species of tree in a single hectare (2.5 acres). Work goes on with ever greater urgency to protect the remaining forests, and 'green' tourism can play a part in underpinning this.

Fringing the coast, the main forest types include the restingas, low growing shrubby thickets which colonize sand-dunes and the Atlantic moist forests, evergreen tropical forests which typically show a four-tiered structure. Coconut palms shade the beaches and mangroves line shallow river-mouths.

The Discovery Coast is so called because it was here, on April 23rd 1500, that the first Europeans stepped ashore in Brazil. A couple of days later, Pedro Álvares Cabral and his company dropped anchor in a deep bay they named Porto Seguro ('safe harbour'). The town of the same name is today one of the most historic in Brazil, and also the headquarters for a

△ *The route follows the beautiful coast*

five-day hike along the coast (equally possible in the opposite direction). Nights are spent in fishing villages, many of which still have no mains electricity, with accommodation in welcoming *pousadas* or guest-houses. The beach-walking is varied by occasional stints along the top of the cliffs (*falésias*), and there are chances to break for paddling or swimming.

After a short ferry crossing and bus ride, the walk starts at Trancoso, originally a Jesuit centre and now something of a hippy colony. The first day is around 24 km (15 miles) to Espelho. It might be worth carrying flippers, mask and snorkel as the beach (Praia do Espelho) has wonderful reefs which, at low tide, can be reached simply by wading.

There's more chance to swim on the second day as it's only 14 km (8.7 miles) to Caraiva, an old fishing village with neither mains electricity nor paved roads. Today it maintains this condition by choice, with cars banished to the other side of the river and modest amenities supported by solar and wind power, attracting eco-chic visitors.

From Caraiva it's an even shorter distance, just 12 km (7.5 miles) to Corumbau, but the day includes the chance to visit the Barra Velha Indian Reservation, at the base of Monte

DESCRIPTION: five days walking along a near-idyllic beach, staying in remote and simple villages

LOCATION: southern Bahia province, Brazil; airport at Porto Seguro

WHEN TO GO: year-round

START: Trancoso, reached by bus and ferry from Porto Seguro

FINISH: Prado

DURATION: 5 days; 110 km (68 miles)

MAX ALTITUDE: virtually all at sea-level

ACCOMMODATION: simple village guest-houses (*pousadas*)

SPECIAL CONSIDERATIONS/EQUIPMENT NEEDED: carry sufficient water and sunscreen. Bring a torch for evenings as villages lack electric light. Snorkel gear (at very least, a mask) is highly recommended

PERMITS/RESTRICTIONS: none

GUIDEBOOK: *The Rough Guide to Brazil* by Dilwyn Jenkins, David Cleary, Oliver Marshall, pb Rough Guides

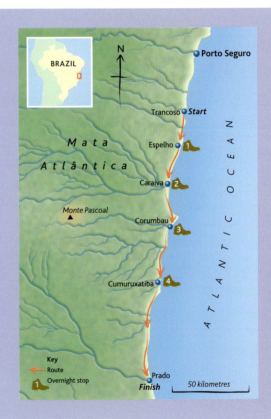

Pascoal, which gave Cabral his first sight of the New World. Here the culture of the Pataxós Indians is maintained and there's a thriving market in traditional handicrafts. Necklaces containing seeds and other natural materials are considered to embody the energy of the natural world.

Corumbau is another traditional fishing village, noted for its fabulous coral reefs. A boat-trip, to see them properly, is hardly to be missed. Again, it would be a great boon to have snorkel gear with you as there's slim chance of renting equipment here.

From Corumbau it's a longer day of 30 km (18.6 miles) to Cumuruxatiba, but with such level walking and plenty of places to rest the distance flows by easily. Along the way is Barra do Cai, a maze of sand-bars at the mouth of the Cai river. Here, Cabral's first landfall is commemorated by a simple wooden cross.

Another longish day leads out to Prado (30 km/18.6 miles) and civilization. It's really a modest town of around 25,000 inhabitants, but can feel like a jumping metropolis after the peaceful ambience of the beach and its villages. Never mind; you could always turn round and walk back again.

▽ *Barro do Cai*

VENEZUELA
Roraima, The 'Lost World'

JON SPARKS

The tepuis of Venezuela are huge, other-worldly table-top mountains ringed by vertical cliffs. The largest, Auyantepui, has an area of over 700 sq km (270 sq miles). Composed of some of the oldest sedimentary rocks in the world, they are sometimes described as islands in time, supporting unique ecosystems. Though Auyantepui is the most extensive of the tepuis, Roraima, 2,739 m (8,986 ft) is the highest. Its summit is the Triple Point where Venezuela, Guyana, and Brazil meet, and is the highest point in Guyana. However, the only feasible ascent is from the Venezuelan side, where there is a single break in the towering cliffs.

This route was followed by the British explorer Sir Everard Im Thurn in 1884 and his account was at least a partial inspiration for Sir Arthur Conan Doyle's classic ripping yarn, *The Lost World*, published in 1912. Its notion of prehistoric creatures surviving on an isolated plateau in turn inspired *Jurassic Park*.

You won't find dinosaurs on Roraima today but you will find a place like nowhere else on earth. Though much of the plateau is bare rock, life takes hold wherever it can. It's reckoned that a third of the plant species on the plateau are found nowhere else. Due to a lack of nutrients in the soil, leached away by the high rainfall, many of the plants are carnivorous.

Contrasting with the clouds and rain that cling to the peak, the initial approach across the Gran Sabana (savannah) is often hot and dry. These grassy plains, dotted with clusters of palms, afford easy walking apart from the crossings of the Tek and Kukenán rivers; straightforward in the dry season, they can require rope protection in the wet. A camp by Rio Kukenán has great views of Roraima and the neighbouring Kukenán-tepui, with its 610 m (2,000 ft) waterfall. A second day's trekking leads to the base of Roraima.

The ascent to the plateau is straightforward, though hard work in the usually hot and sticky conditions. Initially the trail threads through steamy forest, alive with hummingbirds and

▽ *View of Roraima*

festooned with orchids; higher up, the trees give way to primitive tree-ferns. With the sandstone cliffs still looming above and occasional waterfalls spiralling down, it feels ever more like a lost world. Then the trail decants you onto the plateau and a truly alien landscape.

If 'plateau' suggests a flat scene, the reality is anything but; dissected by eons of rain, the ground is a maze of gullies and outcrops. It's hard to get lost on the way to Roraima, but very easy to do so on top. It may only be a tenth of the extent of Auyantepui, but the terrain is convoluted and it's often misty into the bargain.

The weathered rocks also reveal a number of caves and these provide shelter for the camp, usually for a couple of nights. The sandy ground makes a comfortable bed. From this base you can explore the plateau with its innumerable pools, carpets of quartz

facts and figures

DESCRIPTION: easy trekking across open savannah; steep ascent and fascinating exploration of isolated table-land

LOCATION: Parque Nacional Canaima in south-eastern Venezuela

WHEN TO GO: the dry season (November – May) is easiest for trekking, though Roraima can still be wet. The waterfalls, especially Salto Ángel, are of course most impressive in the wet season

START/FINISH: the village of Paraitepui, accessible by rough track (usually 4x4 vehicles only) from main highway

DURATION: 5–6 days

MAX ALTITUDE: 2,739 m (8,986 ft) at summit of Roraima (greater heights often erroneously quoted); average level of the plateau is c 2,500 m (8,200 ft)

ACCOMMODATION: camping; full porter support from the local Pemón people on organised treks

SPECIAL CONSIDERATIONS/EQUIPMENT NEEDED: good breathable waterproof clothing highly recommended!

PERMITS/RESTRICTIONS: it is theoretically possible to go without a guide but it is not recommended

GUIDEBOOK: *Venezuela* by Thomas Kohnstamm *et al.*, pb Lonely Planet

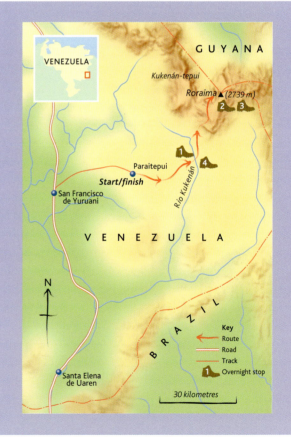

crystals and startling pocket meadows cupped in rocky hollows. It's a fairly full day's round trip if you want to make it all the way to the highest point and that triple frontier, and many visitors prefer to spend the day in a more leisurely fashion, immersing themselves in this astonishing environment. If it's clear, the views from the plateau edge are stunning, but it has to be said that sometimes the clouds never lift. You might even prefer it that way, as the sense of isolation, of being somewhere truly other, is even more palpable.

Slithering down the ramp, back to the plains, you return to civilisation, but chances are you haven't finished with the tepuis yet. The massive Auyantepui spawns the world's highest waterfall, 980 m (3,215 ft) Salto Ángel (Angel Falls) and it's highly likely that a trip to these will be included as part of the package with the Roraima trek. However, reaching them on foot is not really an option and the journey is normally done by boat. Most tourists only see the Salto Ángel from the air, which is impressive enough, but doesn't remotely compare with standing at the base.

◁◁ *Hummingbird perched on a branch, Roraima*

▽ *Hiker on plateau edge of Roraima*

PATAGONIA
Torres del Paine

JASON FRIEND

Patagonia: the very name conjures images of dramatic, awe-inspiring peaks rising out of an open, barren landscape. Considering that this almost mythical region covers the southern expanse of both Argentina and Chile, it is little surprise that there are numerous trekking opportunities available. Some of the area's most famous trails are found within Chile's Torres Del Paine National Park.

▽ *Lago Nordenskjöld*

The 'W' route begins after a brief boat journey to the Lago Grey refuge and campsite. Here it is advisable to pitch your tent or leave any surplus equipment in the refuge before an easy day hike to a viewpoint looking towards the icy façade of Glacier Grey. It can be difficult to fully appreciate the size of this glacier, which forms part of the Southern Patagonian Ice Field, although if you wait a while you will probably witness a sight-seeing boat dwarfed by the towering pillars of blue ice. If time allows, it is recommended to continue approximately three hours past the viewpoint towards the Campamento Paso, where there are magnificent views across the Ice Field towards the distant mountain peaks. Retrace your steps to the Lago Grey refuge where you can spend the night next to a glacier-fed lake complete with floating icebergs.

The next day begins with a steady walk alongside the Lago Grey, heading towards the Lago Pehoé. With luck, the frequent peak-hugging clouds will clear to give a view of the jagged heights of the Paine Grande range, dominating the landscape with a grandeur that far exceeds their elevation. Upon reaching the Pehoé refuge and campsite, the trail doubles back on itself and soon reveals a view of the convoluted massif of the Cuernos del Paine, symbolic of the region. These are the stereotypical Patagonian peaks that have been reproduced in magazines and books throughout the world. The track continues towards the range, alongside the picturesque Lago Skottsberg, where on rare still days the Cuernos del Paine are reflected in the crystal clear waters. Upon reaching the Campamento Italiano, a worthwhile side trip is to head down the Valles Del Frances for impressive views of the Cuernos del Paine and the

△ *Huge crevasses dominate the icy facade of the Grey Glacier*

OVERLEAF *Late afternoon sun illuminates the massif of the Cuernos del Paine*

DESCRIPTION: 4 days' exploring Patagonian valleys in a UNESCO Biosphere Reserve, under the shadows of towering mountain peaks

LOCATION: Torres Del Paine National Park, in the XII region of Chile

WHEN TO GO: November to March, although the weather is unpredictable even in summer and snow is not uncommon

START: Refuge & Camping Lago Grey, reached by bus and ferry combination from Puerto Natales

FINISH: the track finishes at the Hosteria Las Torres, from where scheduled public transport returns to Puerto Natales

DURATION: typically 4 days but extra days should be planned to allow for periods of poor / extreme weather

MAX ALTITUDE: 870 m (2,854 ft) at the Torres Del Paine viewpoint on the final day of the walk

ACCOMMODATION: three nights staying in a refuge or camping within an official park campsite

SPECIAL CONSIDERATIONS: strong wind and snow can be experienced all year round. Accommodation during the summer months can be very busy – reserve a bed before leaving for the park

PERMITS/RESTRICTIONS: there is an admission fee to enter the park

GUIDEBOOK: *Trekking in the Patagonian Andes* by Clem Lindenmayer & Nick Tapp, pb Lonely Planet.

Paine Grande range. Alternatively, continue on the main track, which is a gentle hike towards the azure coloured lake of Lago Nordenskjöld and the refuge and campsite at Los Cuernos.

The penultimate stretch of the route follows the length of the Lago Nordenskjöld, with the track undulating across sun-drenched Patagonian steppe, sandwiched between the Torres range and the lakeside. The surreal form of the Almirante Nieto dominates the skyline as the track follows the outline of the massif before joining the Valle Ascencio. Now the landscape and terrain begin to change dramatically as the route slowly ascends towards the Torres del Paine, finally reaching the Chileno Refuge and campsite.

The final day is both the most arduous and most rewarding. However, it should not be undertaken in poor weather. It is recommended to factor in extra days when planning your trip, to allow you to wait at Chileno for more favorable conditions. Leaving Chileno, the track climbs sharply away from the Ascensio river until it finally rises above the tree line and into an open mountainous landscape. Now the route becomes somewhat more of an endurance test as a vast expanse of huge boulders have to be navigated and climbed to reach a small tarn under the eastern facade of the Torres del Paine. From here the views of the Torres and the surrounding Patagonia landscape are unsurpassed. The Torres themselves are impressive granite towers that appear almost to pierce the sky, rising nearly 2,000 m (6,890 ft) above the tarn. After allowing some time to immerse yourself in the environment, begin a steady descent, finally following the Ascensio River, until you reach the Hosteria Las Torres and the end of your Patagonian adventure.

5 kilometres

Glacier Grey

Campamento Paso

Torres del Paine

Valle Ascencio

Chileno refuge **3**

▲ *Almirante Nieto*

Valles Del Frances

Cuernos del Paine

Hosteria Las Torres **Finish**

Start ○ Lago Grey refuge **1**

Campamento Italiano ○ Los Cuernos **2**

Lago Nordenskjöld

Lago Grey

Lago Skottsberg

N

CHILE

Pehoé refuge ○

Lago Pehoé

Key
→ Route
1 Overnight stop

PICTURE CREDITS

Front cover © Michel Gounot/Godong/Corbis
Back cover: top left © Jon Sparks; top middle © Unlimited Travel; top right © Ronald Turnbull; bottom left © Jon Sparks; bottom right © Jon Sparks

All inside photographs Copyright © Jon Sparks except:

p9 © Adrian Arbib; p53 © Alessandro Saffo/Grand; p21 © Andy Sutton/Alamy; p26, p27, p28-29, p30, p31 © Anthony Toole; p80 © Arthur Morris/Corbis; p124 © Auscape International Pty Ltd/Alamy; p4, p78, p79, p81 © Axel Mertens; p160 © Bill Waldman/Alamy; p160-161 © Jonathan Blair/Corbis; p179 © Brasil2/Istockphoto; p16-17 © Bruce Percy/Alamy; p2, p84-85, p86-87 © Cam Burns; p94 © Charles Philip Cangialosi/Corbis; p33 © Chris Hellier/Corbis; p97 © Chris Lewington/Alamy; p92-93 © Chris Sattlberger/Corbis; p128 © Christian Kapteyn/Alamy; p155 © Christian Klein/Alamy; p132 © Clearvista Photography/Alamy; p130 © Dallas and John Heaton/Free Agents Limited/Corbis; p63 © Danail Marinov/Alamy; p112 © Daniel J. Cox/Corbis; p82 © Danita Delimont/Alamy; p35, p143, p146 © David Pickford; p154 © Douglas Peebles/Corbis; p103© Emma Wood/Alamy; p148 © Frans Lanting/Corbis; p19 © Frantisek Staud/Alamy; p149 © Galen Rowell/Corbis; p184 © Gerrit Buntrock/Alamy; p127 © GM Photo Images/Alamy; p50 © Ilan Rosen/Alamy; p61© Image Register

044/Alamy; p113 © imagebroker/Alamy; p95 © Images of Africa Photobank/Alamy; p74 © ImageState/Alamy; p172 © ImageState/Alamy; p182 © James Sparshatt/Corbis; p170, 186, 187, 188; p171 © Joel Creed; Ecoscene/Corbis; p174 © José Jácome/epa/Corbis; p111 © Keren Su/China Span/Alamy; p42, 43a, 43b, p44, p45, p98, p106, p107, p108 © Kev Reynolds; p176 © Kevin Schafer/Corbis; p126 © LOOK Die Bildagentur der Fotografen GmbH/Alamy; p110 © Marcus Wilson-Smith/Alamy; p90-91 © Michel Gounot /Godong/Corbis; p62 © Nature Photographers Ltd/Alamy; p32 © Owen Franken/Corbis; p10 © Pablo Corral V/Corbis; p142 © Pat O'Hara/Corbis; p129 © Paul Cosgrave www.photoswordspeople.com; p100-101 © Peter Adams Photography/Alamy; p89 © Peter Johnson/Corbis; p185 © Peter M. Wilson/Alamy; p75 © R de la Harpe/Africaimagery; p163© Raymond Gehman/Corbis; p181© Ricardo Funari/BrazilPhotos/Alamy; p175 © Robert Fried/Alamy; p18 © Robert Harding Picture Library Ltd/Alamy; p131© Robert Harding Picture Library Ltd/Alamy; p20 © Roger Noyce; p51 © Roger Ressmeyer/Corbis; p102 © Rolf Richardson/Alamy; p166, 167, 168, 169 © Roly Smith; p64, p65, p66-67, p69, p70, p71, 72, 73 © Ronald Turnbull; p159 © Russ Bishop/Alamy; p162 © Staffan Widstrand/Corbis; p164 © Steve Kaufman/Corbis; p178 © Svea Pietschmann/Alamy; p125, p165 © Tom Till/Alamy; p144, p150, p151, p152, p156 © Tony West; p105 © Travel Ink/Alamy; p83 © Ulrich Doering/Alamy; p88 © Unlimited Travel; p1 © Warren Morgan/Corbis; p177 © Westend 61/Alamy; p76-77 © Winfried Wisniewski/zef; p120 © Galen Rowell/Corbis